UNDERSTANDING BODY LANGUAGE

UNDERSTANDING
BODY
LANGUAGE

HOW TO DECODE
NONVERBAL COMMUNICATION
IN LIFE, LOVE, AND WORK

SCOTT ROUSE

Illustrations by Remie Geoffroi

callisto
publishing
an imprint of Sourcebooks

Copyright © 2021 by Callisto Publishing LLC
Cover and internal design © 2021 by Callisto Publishing LLC
Illustrations © Remie Geoffroi.
Author photo courtesy of Johnathan Jones.
Interior and Cover Designer: Angie Chiu
Art Producer: Sara Feinstein
Editors: Marisa Hines
Production Editor: Matt Burnett

Callisto and the colophon are registered trademarks of Callisto Publishing LLC.

Published by Callisto Publishing LLC C/O Sourcebooks LLC
P.O. Box 4410, Naperville, Illinois 60567-4410
(630) 961-3900
callistopublishing.com

Printed and bound in China
OGP 2

THIS BOOK IS FOR MY
MOTHER AND FATHER.
THANK YOU. FOR ALL OF IT.

CONTENTS

INTRODUCTION

WELCOME TO *Understanding Body Language*! Whether you're just discovering nonverbal communication or you're already an armchair pro, you're going to love this book. We'll start with the basics and go through everything you need to know to make better decisions about the people and situations you deal with every day.

To give you a little background as to why I'm so passionate about understanding human behavior, for the past 51 years I've watched, listened, and studied what every person around me was doing. As a little kid, I wondered why people would be enamored with and drawn to one specific person, while those same people would dread to be around, or even near, another person. Why would my mom correctly have a "wary feeling" about someone who turned out to be bad, before she even talked to them? How could my father, a doctor, tell that a patient was lying to him just by watching them answer his questions? I think I got a pretty good handle on all of that, from the basics to the microscopic details. And since I started so early, I found it easy to explain these complicated things I was figuring out to others.

I'm going to share with you the same information I teach police and military officers, doctors, nurses, mediators, CEOs, entertainers, and entrepreneurs. Of course, some of the things that I teach law enforcement and the military I can't teach you, but I'll cover as much as I can without getting us both in trouble! One thing to keep in mind as you make your way through this book is that there are no "absolutes." That means there are no nonverbal cues that mean the same thing every time you see them. For example, when someone's arms are crossed, it doesn't always mean they are closed off, uninterested, or not listening. They may be cold or just be more comfortable that way.

Finally, before we move forward into the next section in which we map out how to use this book, I'll leave you with one final thought to keep in mind: There are thousands of scientific studies that explain why people do what they do when presented with certain information or situations. That means the body language you see *is* telling you *something*. After reading this book, you'll know what that something is.

HOW TO USE THIS BOOK

GO AHEAD AND TURN TO ANY PAGE in this book and you will learn something. Feel free to! However, the best way to get the most out of the information presented here is to start at the beginning. I will begin slow and small, presenting you with the basics and making sure that you miss nothing. As you learn to recognize the essentials (such as the result of an emotion on someone's face, like deceit, anger, or confidence), you will be able to make better decisions about that person, the situation, and how to address and/or approach them.

You will be practicing what you're learning at home. Sooner than you think, you will naturally begin recognizing cues and tells on the news, on social media, with your friends, and with your family members. You will understand how the body language you're seeing is spoken by everyone you see. Use this as your "warm-up."

Part of that warm-up is being introduced to scenarios similar to those you experience in real life every day. This book has been divided into the various milestones you'll reach. Right out of the gate, we'll focus on this warm-up period. That entails learning how to observe people properly. People don't live in a zoo, so you'll learn to pay attention to what they're doing without drawing attention to yourself. Next stop: practicing on friends and family. Before you head out into the wild, you're going to need some home-based practice time. And who better to observe in their natural habitat than your friends and family?

Our journey into the bowels of human behavior will continue as we suit up for our deep dive into "the good stuff," also known as decoding the hidden messages of dating. Is your date going well or is it headed for the dumpster? Are there key indicators that suggest deceit when your friend claims to have had coffee with a movie star this morning at Starbucks? What parts of the nonverbal breakdown of your date are similar to the situation with your friend? Is it a facial expression? Tone of voice? Something their shoulder did? You will soon recognize how similar each interaction you have is to all the others.

ONE:
UNDERSTANDING THE BASICS

WHAT'S THE REASON for your decision to learn about body language? Do you want to spot lies on true-crime shows? Do you want to understand the nonverbals of the dating scene a little better? Maybe you want to know which politician is actually telling the truth. Maybe you're an entrepreneur who has a pitch coming up and you want to use every tool you can possibly find to help you secure that investment. Or maybe people just fascinate you and you want to learn more about how and why they behave the way they do. Whatever the reason, this chapter is the place to begin.

First, we will talk about the most important skill you'll need to start sharpening and paying close attention to: observation. Before you can learn what to look for concerning nonverbal behavior, you must know *how* to look for it. After that, we'll move on to the nuts and bolts of facial expressions and body language cues so you can begin building your style of observation.

As we go along, you will begin developing your own style of decoding the body language you're observing. Some people are more interested in microexpressions. Others are more interested in the larger cues the rest of the body displays. If you're not sure exactly where your interest lies, that's fine, too. It's not necessary to have a preference.

Take a deep breath. Get that brain of yours opened up. Let's get started.

DRIVING FORCES BEHIND BODY LANGUAGE

For most people, the desire to recognize deception sparks their initial interest in body language and nonverbal communication. With that comes discovering books and blogs and YouTube videos. Your brain becomes a sponge for everything "body language."

As you begin exploring the nonverbal cues and indicators that let you know someone may be lying to you, angry with you, feel contempt towards you, or whatever the case may be, it is important to understand human beings will act and react, from a limbic standpoint, similarly in most situations. In other words, the limbic system—that's the part of the brain that engages your "fight-or-flight" response—will make everyone react pretty much the same way when stimulated. The limbic system does much more than serve as an emergency response, but this is the function we will focus our attention on the most.

When a situation arises stimulating the limbic system into "Protect Mode," sometimes the stimulus is large. For example, a gunshot or someone jumping out of a closet and scaring you. Sometimes the stimulus is small, such as someone asking you about a secret you thought nobody else in the world knew but you.

In the first scenario, when the limbic system is triggered, your brain takes over and immediately and unconsciously moves your arms, hands, and legs into position to protect your heart, throat, and stomach area. It opens your mouth up all the way, so you can breathe quickly and deeply to take in as much oxygen as possible for your muscles, in case you have to fight or run. Your brain also opens your eyes as wide as they will go by raising your eyebrows and lowering your cheeks, so they can take in all the information they can possibly gather in the shortest amount of time concerning the situation.

In the second scenario, your limbic system is triggered, but on a lower level. Your brain isn't under the impression you're in immediate danger, but someone telling you they know your secret can instantly create a stress load that you weren't prepared for. So, you will most likely freeze for a moment. Your pupils will dilate and you won't take your eyes off of that person. You may not even blink. You've been surprised, but not to the level of scenario one. Keep in mind, there's just as much going on in scenario two as in scenario one; however, the average person doesn't know what to look for to catch these much smaller cues. Up to this point in your life, you've seen them all. You just didn't realize what they meant.

Another great example of "the small stuff" you don't realize you see every day was discovered in the late 1800s by French neurologist, Guillaume-Benjamin-Amand Duchenne (also known as Duchenne de Boulogne). Through his experiments in electrophysiology, he discovered there were marked and blatant differences in a real smile and a fake smile. The differences included not only the wrinkles on the outside corners of the eyes that are made during a genuine smile (sometimes called a Duchenne Smile, in his honor), but also *how* they are wrinkled. The same goes for the way the cheeks lift when smiling a real smile. They aren't pushed up by the mouth widening to create a smile; they are pulled up by the brain's reaction to the stimuli. Now that you know this, you will notice it when you see the tiny wrinkles created just under the eyes. When you begin searching for the differences, you will see what Duchenne saw.

We can see small nonverbal cues, or microexpressions, in people's faces when they attempt to hide emotion. That's because the face will "leak" the expression of the specific emotion, despite the person's best efforts to suppress it. Just like the large and small differences in the limbic system's reactions to stimuli, there are similar differences in the large and small reactions of the face when they react to the stimuli of emotion.

(I know this is starting to sound all scientific and horrifically boring, but I have to give you this side of it right at the beginning so you'll have a little background on where the information came from and who discovered it. It's what separates the novice from the

professional when it comes to observation. The boring part is almost over, I promise.)

Once you have absorbed the information in this book and you begin to really observe human behavior for the first time, you will begin to notice what professionals see as red flags and bells and whistles when someone is being dishonest. You will see the cues that differentiate the dishonest person from the person who is just unsure of what they are saying.

The same goes for other emotions that we will cover. Each one can be spotted in their full-blown displays when the person is not trying to conceal them. They can also be seen in microexpression form when there is an attempt to hide them and they leak out. It is important to note that the human face has 43 muscles that control facial expressions. (If you Google this, you'll find there are 42 muscles. They're not counting the tongue, but we're going to.) These 43 muscles can create over 10,000 different facial expressions! However, of the staggering number of expressions, only seven are recognized as being "universal." Universal expressions include Anger, Joy, Sadness, Fear, Surprise, Contempt, and Disgust. They are "universal" because, through research conducted in the late 1960s, Dr. Paul Ekman showed that every culture on Earth exhibits the seven emotions through facial expressions when the correct stimulus is applied, and they mean the same thing to everyone in every culture. Since that time, Dr. Ekman has written 12 books and has become a giant in the study and research of body language with a focus on facial expressions.

Most of the time, Dr. Ekman gets the credit for discovering microexpressions. The truth is, he popularized them, but they were discovered in 1966 by Ernest Haggard and Kenneth Isaacs. They referred to them as "micromomentary expressions." They were looking for cues of nonverbal communication between psychotherapists and their patients by studying their sessions on film in slow motion when they made their game-changing discovery. We won't spend much time in the world of micro-expressions, but it's important for you to have the basic concept under your belt so you can have a proper starting point.

DECEIT

Nonverbal cues of deception exist because the liar's brain must do three things to execute a lie:

1. **STOP THE PERSON FROM TELLING THE TRUTH.** When hearing the question, the limbic system engages. The person decides to lie. You may see their eyes widen slightly and their pupils dilate, and they may take a deeper breath than usual.

2. **CREATE THE LIE.** They need time to think up a believable answer. In some cases, the answer is already prepared. Either way, they need time. So, they might begin the answer with "Well . . ." or "Uhhh . . .", or they may just look at you for a split second too long before answering. You may notice them move back ever so slightly.

3. **DELIVER THE LIE.** There may be a quick one-shoulder shrug or both shoulders may shrug much too quickly. They may lightly nod their head "yes" as they say "no," or vice versa. You're probably under the impression they will break eye contact when lying, but that is not likely. When lying, their brain will want them to keep an eye on you to make sure you believe them.

ANGER

With anger, the first thing you will notice is the person's eyebrows. They will lower and pull toward the center of the brow. Their upper eyelids will be pulled downward as the area just under the eyes is pulled upward. It's a squint of sorts. You may see their teeth clinch and notice the muscles in their jaws flexing every few seconds.

Their lips will stiffen and almost curl inward, sometimes exposing their upper front teeth. Their nostrils will flare, and they will take a deep breath as the limbic system prepares their muscles by giving them more oxygen. Their face may flush for a moment, but that will go away as more blood begins quickly heading toward the muscles in case the person decides to take action.

In the not-so-obvious version of anger, you will notice a much subtler response. The person's nostrils will flare just slightly, while their mouth will close and their lips will tighten. Their eyebrows will come inward a bit and the squint will be much, much smaller than the overt anger response. The person's face may appear flushed. Their breathing may get a bit deeper and stay that way for a longer period of time. Also, as they try to keep the emotion hidden, the volume of their voice may decrease.

HAPPINESS

The telltale signs of happiness are the most pleasant of all facial expressions and behaviors. The person's mouth smiles a wide and real smile, the Duchenne Smile we discussed earlier. With their eyes squinted just the right way to make those little wrinkles on the sides, their cheeks will be pulled up and the dimples at the sides of their mouth will widen and deepen. The volume and tone of their voice may get higher as the person first begins to speak, especially when a gift is involved or a surprise visit or an unexpected meeting is occurring. They may also feel the need to express their happiness with laughs and giddy behavior.

When observing someone who's happy, be sure to pay attention to those in the immediate vicinity. Their expressions will be similar but just a bit subtler. The closer an outside person comes to that group, the more similar their facial expressions will become to those of that group. Their body language cues will also slowly begin to mimic or mirror those in the group.

SUBMISSIVENESS

Submissiveness, anxiety, and lack of confidence can all be displayed with very similar traits and cues. For example, you will see plenty of "adaptors." Adaptors are the small, repetitive behaviors people use to help calm and relax themselves when stress or tension starts to rise. Rubbing their hands together repeatedly or massaging their arm, finger, leg, or neck can have a calming effect. Deep, audible breaths accompany these behaviors.

The person's eyebrows will pull together and push up at the brow. Their posture will usually be bent forward slightly and their shoulders will be drawn inward, depending on the level of anxiety they are feeling. Their head will lean forward and down, and this is sometimes accompanied by rocking back and forth.

Their blink rate will increase. Lack of confidence makes the person want to go unnoticed, so they will unconsciously try to make themselves look smaller. Their feet will tend to point inward when anxious or submissive, and their hands will often be clasped and squeezed between their knees or thighs when sitting. Once you've focused on these behaviors, you'll see them happen quite often out in the wild.

DEPRESSION

Depression can show a wide variety of cues and tells. However, there may also be no signs whatsoever that the person is experiencing any problem. If signs are present, they may include the person sitting still. Their head may be leaned forward and down or sometimes leaned way back on lowered shoulders with a curved posture. It will not be so much that the person is looking straight up, but rather their head will appear cocked back just enough to rest on their shoulders. Their blink rate will be slower, accompanied by a gaze fixed on the floor or a random nearby object.

You will hear their speaking voice is at a much lower volume and tone than usual. There is no lilt or "spark" when they speak or describe something. The gait or pace of their walk will be short and slow. Again, it's important to note that, more often than not, the subtle signs of depression go unnoticed. So, heads up if you think you've spotted two or more of these nonverbal cues.

OPENNESS/CONFIDENCE

We've all seen the confident person. They have great posture; they speak at a good volume—not too loud. They use their hands and arms when they talk. These movements are called "illustrators." This person emphasizes specific words and/or phrases as they tell a story or report information, uses open-handed gestures, and looks you in the eye while they talk.

Cues of confidence can also be found in someone who is happy and/or content with something. Quite often, they will be the first to speak when seeing someone they know or think they know. They will compliment and comment on things positively.

When they walk, they have a wide gait with purpose. This person begins conversations with questions about you and provides positive feedback on whatever you tell them. They use phrases like "you and I" and include "we" and "us" in their conversations.

THE SCIENCE OF BODY LANGUAGE

Experts disagree about theories and science behind human behavior just as much as they concur. However, all agree that everything concerning human behavior is based on the development of the brain.

Science tells us that millions of years ago, when our brains were smaller, one of its most important functions was to keep us safe—from the elements, animals, and every other dangerous situation that early humans could stumble into back then. To make a very long and horrifically boring story short, scientists identified five types of stimuli that, when introduced to the body, trigger behavior:

KINESTHETIC, or touching or feeling the stimuli. For example, if something is too hot or if it pinches your leg or brushes up against you. This includes anything you touch or feel.

VISUAL, or observing the stimuli. For example, a bear running toward you, someone pulling their fist back to hit you, and a car swerving onto the sidewalk toward you. This includes anything you see that can, or is about to, affect you.

AUDIO, or hearing the stimuli. For example, a tiger growling, a shotgun being racked, screeching tires, or bees buzzing. This includes anything you hear that gives you the impression it will, or may, affect you.

OLFACTION, or smelling the stimuli. For example, smoke when you're in a place where there should be none, the odor of natural gas when you walk into your home, or something foul, like dog poop.

TASTE, mainly tasting the stimuli. For example, something sweet versus something sour or bitter. Taste can be combined with kinesthetic stimuli, as the intake may be smooth, crunchy, hot, cold, and/or liquid.

When any of the stimuli under these five categories are introduced, there will be a reaction from the brain. It may be mild or it may be intense, but there will be a reaction. The degree of that reaction depends on the situation the brain is presented with along with the stimuli.

For example, if you're absorbed in a book, reading quietly, and your friend sneaks up behind you and grabs your head and screams, your limbic system will trigger a full-blown reaction of surprise. You will probably make a noise similar to someone being shocked with a cattle prod. Your arms will come together to protect your stomach, heart, and lungs as your brain pulls your shoulders up and your head forward and down to attempt to protect your neck. Your knees will come up quickly to protect your reproductive organs. You can't help but do this. You're not in control of it. Your brain—or more specifically, your limbic system—is reacting.

The same reaction will happen with anyone exposed to the same or similar stimulus or scenario. This is the result of an inborn, universal reaction. We're all going to do it. It's an "inborn" reaction because we're all born with a limbic system to protect us and it makes us all react that way. (Again, there are a few exceptions, but let's continue keeping it simple.) And since every one of us will react that way, it's a "universal" reaction.

Let's say something similar happens. You're reading and you're deep in thought. However, this time you're sitting on a bench under a large tree. Hang on a second . . . You hear an odd noise. Then you recognize that noise is a cracking sound. The sound is above you. You realize it's the sound of a tree limb cracking and you react. Your brain has gone through a processing protocol and it said, "Hey, I know that cracking sound means there's a large tree limb breaking. It's above me and it might hit me. I'd better move right now, so I don't get killed!"

Your hands let go of the book as you push off the bench, and you run as fast as you can away from the tree. You may even fall forward to the ground as you turn to make sure you've escaped the threat. This behavior is a combination of a learned reaction and a limbic reaction. Logic tells your brain what is happening and to get away from the tree. As you moved away, your limbic system once again brought your shoulders up and your head forward and down to protect your neck as your hands and arms came together and forward to protect your stomach, heart, and lungs.

A baby would have no idea what was happening if it were in that situation. It probably wouldn't move at all. That's because it hadn't learned the sequence of events that follow the sound of that cracking limb. However, put the baby in the first scenario we talked about, and it would react similarly to the way you did. Again, that's an inborn, universal reaction.

One of the greatest examples of the differences in inborn and universal cues compared to the learned cues can be found when learning about facial expressions. As Paul Ekman proved in his research, there are seven universal facial expressions that have the same meaning no matter what culture they are found in.

From Sweden to Turkey, Milan to Papua New Guinea, the expressions of Anger, Joy, Sadness, Contempt, Fear, Surprise, and Disgust convey the same meanings no matter who you're talking to. All other facial expressions, although they may have similar meanings, indicate something different.

The ability to differentiate an inborn cue from a learned cue is important because it lets us know what the person we're talking to or observing is really thinking and/or feeling. If we see an inborn/universal cue when we are asking an important question, we are seeing the true reaction of that person's brain to the stimulus of the question. If we see what we know is a learned cue, it doesn't mean they're being dishonest; it means they are showing us the reaction they want us to see.

CULTURAL VARIATIONS

As the Entrepreneur in Residence at the Nashville Entrepreneur Center from 2011 to 2017, I taught new entrepreneurs and startups how to create investable pitches to get funding for their ideas. The body language and nonverbals I would train them to use were paramount in winning trust and credibility with their investors. To this day, every entrepreneur I've worked with and trained has been funded—not just 10, 20, or 50 startups, but hundreds, from Nashville to Silicon Valley and beyond. By teaching them the same nonverbal cues you're already learning in this book, I've helped startups raise well over $400 million in funding.

While working with the Entrepreneur Center, I developed an online course that was used by over 3,500 entrepreneurs around the world that helped them create a pitch and use specific body language to help get the funding they needed. Since the entrepreneurs who took the online course were from so many different countries, there had to be an explanation and breakdown of the differences in the cultural and limbic body language issues and cues they would see and use in different countries.

An example of these types of cultural variations occurred a few years ago, when there was a startup from Silicon Valley that I worked with. They had a great idea, focused on robotics and AI. The CEO, Maria, was Bulgarian and the CFO, Yiannis, was Greek. We worked together well as a team and eventually were successful in obtaining the investment they were asking for. However, it did not occur without a couple of major hiccups during our first meeting.

At the first meeting, we met in an attorney's office on the twelfth floor of a high-rise in downtown Nashville. The attorney representing them was a friend of mine and let me know a few things about each of them ahead of time. One bit of information shared was that the parties lived close to each other in San Francisco and both had "significant others." As I began my initial "sweep" for deception using small talk and asking simple questions, I was getting what I thought was a pretty good baseline on both of them. Then I started asking questions I already knew the answers to.

I asked Maria, "So, you two live in San Francisco, huh?" She smiled and said, "Yes," as she shook her head. "Yiannis has been there longer than I have." I immediately turned to Yiannis and asked him, "Do you two live together?" He shook his head slightly and said, "No. We live close to each other though. I live with my girlfriend and Maria has a fiancé." I turned to Maria and said, "Yeah?" while nodding my head, and she said, "Yeah," while shaking her head.

At this point, I've got alarm bells going off telling me something isn't right here. She's saying "No" and "Yes," while her nonverbals are telling me the exact opposite. His nonverbals all seem fine to me. I've seen this before, though: A con running a game where the partner has no idea they're involved with anything questionable.

Keep in mind, I've dealt with more con artists than I can count, and this was starting to give me that same old "this might be a con" feeling I always get. The more yes or no questions I asked, the more she answered "Yes" with her head nods and "No" with her words, then "No" with her head shakes and "Yes" with her words. They said they had known each other for almost seven years. Had they met just in the last few months? Why all the incongruence with her body language when answering these simple questions? Maybe there's a side relationship between them going on, or something like that.

Then I asked Maria, "Did you use the stairs to get up here?" Keep in mind we were in an office on the twelfth floor with a great view of downtown Nashville. She laughed and said, "No, of course not!" All the while, she nodded her head "Yes." Then it hit me. In Bulgaria, they shake their heads "No" for "Yes" and nod their heads "Yes" for "No." Dang it, I knew this! They do the same thing in Albania. Most people are under the impression that the head nod "Yes" has the same meaning all over the world. Though it does mean the same thing in Africa, China, the Middle East, and Western Europe, there are many places where it means the exact opposite.

"Where are you from?" I asked Maria. "Bulgaria," she replied. Then I started laughing out loud. "Why is that so funny? Do you have a problem with Bulgarians?" Yiannis asked. "Oh no!" I laughed, "That's not it at all, I promise, everything is fine." As I said, "Everything is fine," I gave him a small but quick thumbs-up.

Before I could say, "I finally understand why her nonverbal behavior wasn't doing what I thought it should be doing," Yiannis stood, his nose crinkled, his lips pursed and turned inward, and his brow furrowed. I knew this combination all too well. This guy was going to take a swing at me. "Hang on! Hang on!" I yelled as I stood up and put my hands up in front of me. "Hear me out!"

To make a long story short, I flipped him off. By using the thumbs-up gesture, I accidentally shot him the Greek version of "the bird." This same rule goes for Sardinia and Iran. In West Africa and some parts of South America, it translates to "Up yours!" In Brazil, it means "Thank you." That just goes to show you how important it is to stay engaged when making decisions about whether you are seeing limbic or cultural behavior in someone's reactions to situations or questions.

When you hear an Indian accent and ask that person a question, and they answer while shaking their head from side to side, that is the equivalent of the up and down shake that denotes "Yes" for most everyone else.

In Greece, they signify "Yes" with a head tilt to the left and then to the right. They signify "No" by tilting the head up and back. In Yiannis's case, he had lived in the United States since he was a child and had no problems with the American version of "Yes." However, his family still used the thumbs-up gesture as one of aggression.

BEST PRACTICES AND TIPS FOR SUCCESS

There is nothing I enjoy more than hanging out with another expert in human behavior, and Greg Hartley is my favorite partner to hang with. Greg is a former US Army interrogator, trainer, and body language expert. He is also a successful author and one of the "Big Guns" of the body language world. We've spent hours sitting in restaurants watching people, deciding what's happening with them, and betting on what they're going to do next.

The restaurant setting is one of *the* best places to begin your journey observing human behavior. That's because you see so many different people from so many different walks of life and they will react almost the exact same way when the waitperson comes to the table for the first time. They will also react similarly when giving their orders. The same goes for when they spot the food heading toward their table.

Behavior when summoning and receiving the check is my personal favorite. As the waitperson arrives, you'll sometimes see diners "fight" for the check. If you pay close attention, you'll easily figure out who attempts to lose that battle. As you learn more and get in deeper, you'll be able to spot the cues of stress on the person who doesn't want to pay, and you'll spot the smallest frustration and/or disappointment cues on the person who knows it's not their turn but pays anyway.

The next time you're in a restaurant, pick a table and watch the hands of the people at that table. That's all—just their hands. In the first few seconds, you will notice each person exhibiting similar behaviors. As they settle in, some will have their elbows on the table and lean in, and some will have their hands on their laps. Some will goof around with their phone for a bit. As the first few minutes pass and the server comes to the table to greet them, you will notice each person begin to match and mimic the others' postures and behaviors. But remember, you're just watching hands right now.

As someone speaks, you will see them begin using illustrators. They will usually start small and, as they become more comfortable, they will grow larger. Pay attention to the hands of those listening. Where are they? What are they doing? This is where you're going to find out if you are truly interested in learning about human behavior. If you are, you'll find yourself saying, "Holy smokes . . . That happens every time he does . . .," or, "The people at this table are doing the EXACT same things the people at that table were doing four minutes ago!" You'll know you simply have a passing interest if after five minutes you say, "Yeah, no. I'm not seeing anything here."

As you develop your new skill set, you will settle into your own style of decoding nonverbal behavior. Quite often, a person's interest in facial expressions ignites their want to learn more about body language and what it will tell them. That's where most start to break down what they're seeing.

Although decoding facial expressions is a great starting point, the problem is, you can't necessarily start there every time. For example, what can you pick up from the nonverbals of the person with their back to you in line at Target? In this scenario, you can't see their face. All you can see is the back of their head, the backs of their feet, arms, legs, and torso. Where do you begin?

Start big and work your way to the smaller things. For example, are they standing still or slowly swaying back and forth? Swaying indicates boredom. What's their posture like?

Are they leaning on a shopping cart? If so, this tells us they don't feel threatened by anything going on around them. What about their head? Is it straight up? Most often, this denotes they are paying attention. Is the head leaning to one side and back? That suggests impatience. What are their arms doing? Are they crossed? This could mean they're cold, bored, exasperated with the situation, or just more comfortable with crossed arms.

Where are their hands? What are they doing? Are they fidgeting with something? The fidgeting denotes they are thinking about something specific. Are they holding their phone with one hand and "paddling" it between the middle finger and thumb of the opposite hand? This suggests they want things to speed up a bit. Are they holding a shopping basket in front of them with both hands while leaning back and their head is back as well? Again, this denotes boredom. If they're holding the basket with one hand, what's the other hand doing? Written out, you could get the impression that learning all this will take quite some time. However, you will soon be able to decode everything in this situation within a few seconds.

If you are in a much closer position and can see it, then start with the face. Are the lips pursed? That suggests disagreement with the situation. Are they pursed to the side? That indicates the person sees a different outcome to what is happening or what just happened. Have their lips disappeared by curving inward, so you can't see them? You'll see this when someone is stressed or when their stress level is building.

As you observe someone out in the wild, ask yourself these three questions:

1. **IS EVERYTHING AS IT SHOULD BE FOR THIS PARTICULAR SITUATION?**

2. **IS THIS PERSON'S BEHAVIOR TELLING ME SOME-THING IS WRONG OR THAT THERE IS AN ISSUE?**

3. **IS THEIR BEHAVIOR TELLING ME EVERYTHING IS OKAY?**

If everything looks normal, search for small adaptors, such as massaging an arm or hand, biting a lip, pulling on or biting fingernails, or repetitive mouth movements or noises.

While searching for small adaptors, you may begin to notice that they are growing larger. For example, someone may quickly shrug their shoulders to stretch those muscles and help them relax. They may squeeze and wipe their forehead quickly or continuously rub a finger. You may hear them take a deep breath and let it out louder than normal. The adaptors a person uses, whether large or small, tell you something isn't right for them psychologically. As ex-FBI agent Joe Navarro puts it, "You're looking for the adjustments in comfort and discomfort." That's what adaptors do: aid in the transition from comfort to discomfort and vice versa.

TWO:

WARMING UP

YOU DON'T HAVE TO LOOK FAR to begin observing human behavior: Just take a look at your phone. Name it and you will most likely see that type of behavior on social media sometime today. You will see a marked difference in the people who are doing things in hopes that their video will go viral and the people who are just standing around being recorded and don't care or know that it's happening.

For example, while someone is doing something that they think is funny or clever, they will not only talk louder, but their illustrators and adaptors will be "louder" as well. You will see larger movements of their arms and legs. Their facial expressions will be much more defined than normal. Their movements will be quicker, and their attention will be concentrated on the camera. With the sound muted, it will seem as though their entire body is trying to tell you something.

You can make these same comparisons observing normal and amped-up behaviors when you're watching the news and an excited person is being interviewed. The same goes for when a local politician is angry because the *whatever it is* still hasn't been addressed yet—or maybe election time is right around the corner.

Now that you have a grip on the basics of nonverbal communication, you will be able to start making decisions about the behaviors you see politicians and salespeople exhibit on TV and social media. Now let's take a look at some specific cues to look for.

START OUT WITH SOCIAL MEDIA

Confidence shows in a person's behavior when they appear to be calm with little or no distracting or jerky movements, especially when you pay attention to their head. You'll notice that when you observe people with a large following on social media. News anchors and talk show hosts also look and act this way. Although some of their movements will be larger than normal, that's part of the art of keeping the viewer's attention.

In the image on page 24, you can see what we call "open" gestures and body language. The hands are visible and you can see the stomach, chest, and neck easily. These cues suggest the host is not feeling threatened or stressed.

If you were watching him talk, you would notice that his vocal tone and diction would be clear and projected at a good volume. He wants to get every word across so that the listener misses nothing. He *must* keep the viewers' attention and keep them excited, no matter what is happening. These same principles apply for a video featuring someone that has a large social media following. They're doing it to get a message across, and capturing and keeping attention is of the utmost importance. The bigger moves are important here.

As you learn more, you'll find yourself migrating to the same cue areas as you observe. It may be the face, where you will first focus on the eyes, mouth, and facial expressions. It may be the hands, where you will search for the small adaptors first. For some, it's the middle of the torso. That helps get a quick assessment of cues that are normal as well as out of place, starting big and working toward the small. This is the process of settling into your "style" of decoding. Now let's get a closer look and break down some of the classic cues you'll see a lot.

01
Hand Gesturing

03
No Movement
of Eyebrows
and Forehead

04
Showtime
Smile

02
Large Torso
Movements

05
Hand Lightly
Touching Table

UNDERSTANDING BODY LANGUAGE

01: HAND GESTURING

Hand gestures are one of the most important tools in a talk show host's body language toolbox. They fall into two categories. The first is the illustrator category, which we will talk about in-depth soon. The second is the regulator category. Regulators help direct attention, move things forward, slow things down, speed things up, or even bring everything to a stop.

One-on-one, hand gestures are usually small and stay within the stomach and lower chest area. It's rare to see someone gesturing above the shoulders as in this illustration. However, sporting events are one place where you may see both hands raised above the head and shoulders, or gesturing above the shoulders.

When speaking to a group, the gestures *need* to be larger and have more movement. The same principle applies for video and film. The larger the movements, the more there is to see and the more the viewer's attention is attracted to or directed by the person executing the gestures. Here we see an open-handed gesture indicating the host is asking for an answer or suggestion.

02: LARGE TORSO MOVEMENTS

Talk show hosts are seated. That means the ability to make large movements and gestures—things like walking away, spinning around, going down on one knee, bowing forward, and all of the more dramatic movements you can make when you are standing—are out of the question. That's why you will see much larger movements in the torso area as the host acts and reacts humorously, seriously, doubtfully, and confidently.

Instead of standing straight and bowing their head when there is a somber moment, the host will sit up straight and bow their head. When given interesting, questionable, or greatly anticipated information, their torso will tilt forward.

When given unexpected news, graphic information, or bad news, their torso will tilt back, to the side, or both. Depending on the type, importance, and degree of unpleasantness, this movement may happen faster or slower. In the seated position, the torso has the ability to bring the head, face, and chest closer to the guest or take it further away. These large torso movements are imperative in keeping and directing the viewer's attention.

03: NO MOVEMENT OF EYEBROWS AND FOREHEAD

There's no doubt about it: Botox has become more popular, as well as more accessible, over the past few years. Many people, including some celebrities, use it to help get rid of wrinkles in the forehead and brow area. And while it can make a big difference, there are consequences. For example, if a host is showing cues that suggest he is eliciting an answer, like "What do you think?" then his eyebrows should be up. Greg Hartley refers to that as a "request for approval." In this instance, though he is requesting approval or an answer, the eyebrows are not pushed or pulled upward. The forehead is motionless and is not wrinkling. This suggests Botox has been used.

Some people can be expressive enough with the rest of their face, as is the case with this host, in which case Botox use isn't problematic. News anchors can take advantage of the effect and continue to look serious even though the story they are relaying may be sad or even a bit humorous, but the eyebrows and forehead play important roles in connecting with others. It's a big chance to take if you're a person whose livelihood depends on that connection.

04: SHOWTIME SMILE

The smile is the most pleasant and popular facial expression. The logic goes, the bigger the smile, the happier the person. That might be true, but only if the person is displaying a real, genuine smile. Having been a record producer for many years, I learned plenty from the artists I worked with, especially when it comes to an artist's behavior while performing.

The most common behavior you will see onstage—whether you're observing a musician, actor, keynote speaker, or talk show host—is their smile. When you see one of these smiles, most often you're seeing that person's "Showtime Smile."

The Showtime Smile is practiced and rehearsed, and it looks exactly the same every time you see it. Take a look at photos of your favorite celebrity on the red carpet. They will display plenty of smiles there. Then take a look at that same celebrity on the red carpet from another event. See it? The exact same smile.

Now that you're aware of this, pay attention to your own smile. Is it the smile you really want history to record when your picture is taken? It's okay to practice your smile. Believe me, more people practice theirs than you're aware of!

05: HAND LIGHTLY TOUCHING TABLE

When someone places their complete attention on one person or situation, they become loosely unaware of what the rest of their body is doing. It's not that they have no idea what the rest of their body is doing; they have simply put most of their attention somewhere else. Pickpockets, magicians, and con artists depend on that loosely unaware state to steal your wallet or take advantage of you. That's why the host's hand is placed so oddly on the desk. They are completely focused on the audience. You do this as well, when you are in situations demanding your undivided attention.

One time, at camp, when I was very young, the archery champ from a local college came to show us how to use a bow and arrow. She was incredible. She would take her time, draw the arrow back as she aimed, and let the arrow fly flawlessly every time. As she began one of her shots, a honeybee landed on her face. On her face! And she didn't so much as flinch. She made the shot, realized there was a bug on her face, and swiped it off. I will never forget that level of concentration. She experienced, to a much greater degree, what the host is experiencing in the illustration.

THE HIDDEN ART TO POLITICS

You may be under the impression that decoding the body language of politicians is tough because their movements are so big and rehearsed. In reality, those are the factors that make politicians so much easier to read than a normal person. It's the same reason comedians can easily imitate them. Their behaviors are so rehearsed and so big, yet so personalized.

Politicians are great to study, because they are always available to watch and observe. They are always on TV and social media. They put out videos about where they stand on whatever issue is currently being discussed. Someone is always interviewing them. You don't realize what a great behavioral baseline you already have on many politicians today because you've seen and heard them talk and answer so many questions so often.

When watching a politician being questioned or accused, it is imperative to keep your mind open. Just observe. Before they are asked the big question or questions, pay attention to their face. Is it focused on the interviewer? How loud and how clearly are they speaking? Is there movement in their head, shoulders, arms, hands, and/or torso? Are the movements big or small?

What kinds of words are they using? How fast are they talking? Are they using any adaptors? Are the pauses longer than normal for that politician? Is the answer they are giving the answer to the question they were asked? If it's a yes or no question, did they answer with a "Yes" or a "No"? Or was it a long answer that really didn't go anywhere? These are all simple and easy to spot.

One of the first things you learned in this book was that there are no absolutes. That means you cannot see only one of the things we discuss here and assume the politician is lying. If you see two of them, you can't assume they are lying. If you see three of them? Then you can say, "Hang on a second . . . Something's not right here. Let's watch that again."

If the behavior you know as normal for this politician hasn't deviated since the interview began and their demeanor stays calm or remains low-key, that indicates low stress and the answers are most likely truthful. However, if the illustrators start popping up or become larger and/or the tone of their voice and facial expression changes, keep watching. Something's up.

It's decision time. Are they becoming more animated because they are excited about the question or subject and can't wait to tell you what they think? Or are you watching them become anxious, restless, or uncomfortable because they're getting ready to answer untruthfully? As the adaptors pile up, the chances that a lie is marching its way toward the conversation grows greater.

As a soon-to-be impeached President Clinton told America he was innocent of the accusations against him, we saw his face change, his adaptors change, and his tone of voice change. We saw his body language go from comfortable to uncomfortable.

01
Talking in One
Direction While
Pointing in Another
Direction

03
Blink Rate Slows

04
Single-Shoulder
or Short Shrug

02
Hand Gestures
Out of Sync with
Emphasized Words

05
Hand Gripping
the Podium

01: TALKING IN ONE DIRECTION WHILE POINTING IN ANOTHER DIRECTION

Illustrators are used when a person wants to emphasize specific words or phrases as they speak. For example, when President Clinton denied having a sexual relationship with Monica Lewinsky, he said, "I did not have sexual relations with that woman." As he said that, he tapped the podium with his finger on the words NOT-HAVE-SEXUAL-RELATIONS. He was focused and paying full attention to what he was doing and saying. This phrase was well-rehearsed, as was his use of illustrators.

When giving an honest answer, the illustrators will be gesturing at or toward the person being given the answer. In this press conference, President Clinton was looking at and speaking to Wolf Blitzer, but he was gesturing to the far right of Wolf. This suggested something wasn't right with his answer.

Using illustrators doesn't mean a person is lying, nor does it mean that an individual is telling the truth. It is simply a way for the person to make sure those listening understand that there are certain parts of what they are saying that are extra important.

02: HAND GESTURES OUT OF SYNC WITH EMPHASIZED WORDS

Although President Clinton's famous finger point-ing illustrators were actually pointing in the wrong direction the first time he used them, they tapped in sync with the words NOT-HAVE-SEXUAL-RELATIONS.

The second time he used illustrators, they stood out like a sore thumb. The reason being that they were not in sync with the words as they were spoken. If the brain is focused on and emphasizing specific words and phrases, then those illustrators *must* be in sync with those words and phrases. If not? Something is definitely wrong.

This doesn't necessarily denote lying. The person could be thinking about something else at the same time they are speaking, or there may be something else going on in the background or foreground that is pulling their attention away. Remember, there are no absolutes in body language.

However, whenever I see and hear illustrators that aren't in sync with the words they're supposed to be emphasizing, I pay closer attention to that person's answers.

03: BLINK RATE SLOWS

You may have heard, "When someone is lying, their blink rate will increase." That does prove true in some cases. For example, if the person is being interrogated or is being questioned for more than just a couple of minutes, that will most likely cause the limbic system to kick in. In these cases, their eyes will dry a bit and they will blink at a faster rate.

However, after a person gives information they know to be false but want to be believed, their blink rate actually slows down. That's because the brain tries its best to keep an eye on the person being lied to in an attempt to gauge whether they are buying the lie. That's what can be seen in President Clinton's behavior.

In the twelve seconds it takes to deliver the lie, he blinks 12 times. That's a rate of 1 blink per second. After he says "These accusations are false," it's another 7 seconds before he blinks again, even though he also says, "And I need to go back to work for the American people." He scans the room making sure those people believe him.

04: SINGLE-SHOULDER OR SHORT SHRUG

You see shoulder shrugs all the time. When you ask a question and the person doesn't know the answer, they'll probably shrug their shoulders as they say "I don't know." That's normal. A real shoulder shrug lasts about a second, sometimes a second and a half. However, if you see a really quick shoulder shrug or just a one-shoulder shrug, there's probably an issue there.

That's because, as they answer the question, the brain is in that loosely unaware state we talked about earlier. They are focused on you and your question, and they don't realize that what they think is a full-on shoulder shrug is just a quick pop up and down that most don't even notice.

Pretend someone is asking you the question, "Who is Mackland Dan Vanderboots?" When you answer, shrug your left shoulder. See how unnatural that feels? It looks unnatural as well. Now pretend you're asked that question and make both shoulders shrug quickly. Again, it looks as unnatural as it feels. When you see it, there's most likely an issue there.

05: HAND GRIPPING THE PODIUM

When something is happening and a person wants to make sure they have stable footing, they will hold on to something and brace themselves. You may see that same behavior when a person is bracing to get news or give news. That's what you're seeing in the illustration: President Clinton grips the podium here to brace himself.

Is this an adaptor? Yes. His index finger is pushing hard on the outside of the podium as the rest of his fingers form a grip. His forearm is pushing on the podium, as well as the rest of his arm close to his side. The arm at his side denotes his limbic system is in protection mode, guarding his stomach and chest area.

What does him being so close to the podium tell us? It tells us he is using it as a barrier. It's normal to be a few inches back from the podium. It's not normal to be almost pressing against it. Every piece of behavior in this illustration tells us he is guarded, stressed, and preparing to deliver questionable information.

THREE:
PRACTICING ON FRIENDS AND FAMILY

MOST OF THE NONVERBAL communicating you do with friends and family typically goes unnoticed. You're around them so much that you don't realize that you are reacting to the smallest of head nods or eyebrow movements. Your family members also probably completely miss the fact that they are reacting to your subtle mouth, arm, and chin movements.

On the other hand, there are plenty of things you do notice, like the quick grimace on the face of your significant other when you mention a certain someone from work. Even though they are under the impression that you didn't see that grimace, you know it's better not to ask that certain someone from work to the barbeque next Saturday.

The same thing goes when you're shopping for clothes and you have a friend with you. You walk out of the dressing room and say "Well? What do you think?" Their response is "Yeah, that works for you," but their squirmy body language says, "Actually, it makes you look hilarious, but I know you like it so I'm not going to say anything."

You know what that slow release of breath you just heard from your best friend means. You know it's time to talk about what's bothering them. You know what it means when you and your brother run into one of his classmates and his eyebrows raise and stay up the entire time he's talking to her. It's time for you to say, "Hey, I'll meet you at the car." When you know someone very well, you know their nonverbal cues and tells, even though you don't realize it.

HOW TO READ SOCIAL GATHERINGS

Social gatherings are fascinating, as they put every participant's behavior on display. You can spot the shy, the nervous, and the fake. Connecting properly with these people is much easier when you know where their heads are at from a nonverbal perspective.

Approach the shy person in a quieter fashion and compliment them on something they're wearing or something they've said. They are easily spotted, as quite often they will exhibit shrugged shoulders and/or their hand or hands will be in their pocket(s). Their feet are usually fairly close together as well. Understand you're going to be doing the heavy lifting in the conversation and know that that's okay. The questions you ask them can begin in a similar way to those you would ask an introvert, such as questions about the things we all do at home. "Have you binge-watched that show yet?" Or, "What book are you in the middle of?" "Are you a dog person or a cat person?" works like a charm with shy people.

Connecting with the nervous person the right way will be a little harder. They are processing a whole lot more that's going on and in a different way than you are. It's important to be patient with them and to speak calmly and clearly. You might notice adaptors, larger ones like arm massaging, shaking a leg, rubbing a hand. They may even have a tight grip on their cup or glass. Taking a deep breath, letting it out audibly and saying "Sometimes these things are too much" can help them under-stand that you get it. If that doesn't help, you might try smiling and saying, "You look like how I feel." When they say, "How's that?" or, "What does that mean?" you can say, "I just don't like these things. I know everybody else does, and I should, but I just don't like 'em." You will be surprised how that can calm a nervous partygoer.

The person exhibiting a "fake front" is usually the most interesting. You'll know them by the loud volume they speak at.

Their head will probably be tilted back, almost like they're looking down their nose at you. They may have one hand on their hip and their chest forward a bit as well, while at the same time having one of their legs sticking out in front of them just a little too far. Though showing many signs of a narcissistic attitude, they may be faking that front of confidence to hide the fact that they are sad, nervous, unsure, or even shy. Approach this person

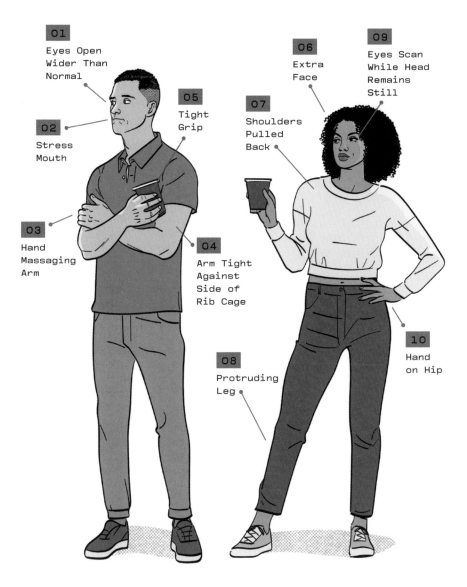

01
Eyes Open
Wider Than
Normal

02
Stress
Mouth

03
Hand
Massaging
Arm

05
Tight
Grip

04
Arm Tight
Against
Side of
Rib Cage

06
Extra
Face

07
Shoulders
Pulled
Back

09
Eyes Scan
While Head
Remains
Still

10
Hand
on Hip

08
Protruding
Leg

with a bit of caution, as some of the cues are similar to those of a con or grifter. The person who is truly confident will rarely exhibit more than one or two of the several cues you can spot with these people. A great opening line for the person you suspect of being fake is: "So, what is your take on all of this?" This type of person will usually answer with information based more on them and much less on what is going on at the party.

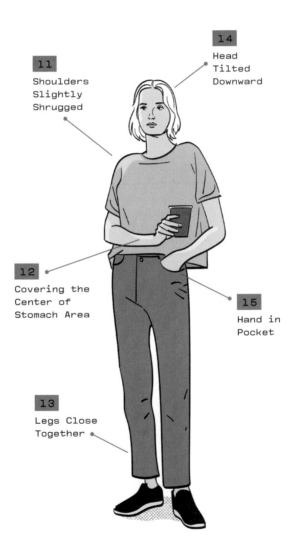

14
Head
Tilted
Downward

11
Shoulders
Slightly
Shrugged

12
Covering the
Center of
Stomach Area

15
Hand in
Pocket

13
Legs Close
Together

01: EYES OPEN WIDER THAN NORMAL

The nervous person's brain wants to take in as much information as it possibly can from its surrounding environment. They tend to check the surroundings every couple minutes or so, and they listen to everything more closely than most other people.

To aid their ability to process this deluge of constantly changing information, the limbic system is triggered and the brain makes sure the eyes are open a little wider than they normally would be. They aren't wide enough to look odd, but wide enough to be noticeable.

The nervous person will go back and forth between a higher state of alert to a lower state, over and over, in an observable cycle. If you notice this cycle, it is best to engage the person while they're in the lower alert state. They will be much easier to approach and more open to listening to and engaging with you. They will also appreciate someone "coming to the rescue" as they try to cope with whatever is bothering them.

02: STRESS MOUTH

When there's a problem or when a person is stressed, quite often you will see what we like to call "Stress Mouth." Some refer to it as "Lip Compression," while others call it "Disappearing Lips." The person's lips will push together from the top and bottom and curve inward, until it looks like they've disappeared. You'll see this in almost every courtroom, especially when the ethics of the person in the hot seat are in question.

Stress Mouth can show up during different levels of stress. For example, when you're at a party and you walk out of the kitchen or into the living room and see people you don't know, if someone looks you in the eye as you pass and smiles, your lips will try to smile. They'll press together and disappear as you nod your head at the person. You'll probably do the same thing if you're sitting at a red light on the way home and realize the person you're looking at in the car next to you is staring back.

03: HAND MASSAGING ARM

One of the most common pacifiers you will see are a person massaging their arm, hand, finger, or a shoulder. We most often employ these pacifying behaviors as we deal with a problem or situation we are uncomfortable with.

I was giving a TEDx Talk in Nashville and there were several talks scheduled throughout the day. I headed over a little early to get a look at the venue, to see how large the audience was, and to get used to the surroundings.

As I stood in the back watching another speaker being introduced, a friend of mine stepped up and said, "Hey, is your arm okay?" I didn't realize I was massaging my arm so hard that it looked like I was trying to pull it off. I was nervous because there were almost 2000 people in the audience and I was only expecting around 500.

As I unconsciously tried to calm myself, I was employing the classic self-pacifying arm massage. When you see someone exhibiting this behavior, more often than not, the person has no idea they're doing it.

04: ARM TIGHT AGAINST SIDE OF RIB CAGE

One of the important things the limbic system does is protect us when we sense something is wrong. When this response is triggered, without realizing it, our arms spring immediately to our sides with our forearms and hands in front of our stomach, chest, and heart. At the same time, our face exhibits the expression of Surprise: eyes and mouth wide open, eyebrows pulled up, nostrils flared, and pupils dilated.

The facial expression of Fear is similar to Surprise, in that the expression of Fear looks like a calm Surprise. In a way, it's the same with Anxiety, which is related to Fear. Anxiety has some of the hallmarks of the miniaturized facial expression of Fear, so there are some similar cues and tells you can pick up on and use here.

In this illustration, the nervousness is largely cued by how tightly the arm is pressed against the rib cage. As the environmental pressure increases and decreases, the arm serves as an adaptor to aid in releasing stress and tension building up inside the person.

05: TIGHT GRIP

During the first drop on a roller coaster, you don't lightly touch the shoulder harness that keeps you in your seat. Your hands squeeze that harness like it's the only thing keeping you alive. Again, your limbic system is protecting you, forcing you to hang on tight.

If you see someone at a party holding their glass about chest level, pay attention to their grip. Are they holding it lightly? Or tightly, like a new comedian holding a microphone during their first appearance on a late-night talk show? Along with one or two other adaptors, you will see the tightness of a person's grip is an adaptor as well. A tight grip is also used as a barrier when it's at that chest-height level. A barrier can be anything placed between you and another person.

Similar to crossed arms during an uncomfortable conversation, a person with a tight grip on a glass, coffee cup, or other object held in front of their heart and chest area can indicate anxiety and/or fear.

06: EXTRA FACE

My brother is in the TV and movie business. Once, I visited him on the set of a show he was directing. Every so often, he would yell "Cut!" and he would ask the extras to "stop making that weird face." After hearing him say that so often, I asked, "What's that about?" He replied, "When a scene starts, look at the faces of the extras. Some will put this odd-looking smile on their face when they hear 'Action!' They do that because they know they're on camera."

Ever since he pointed that out, I can't stop looking for it. Now, I see "Extra Face" everywhere in movies, sitcoms, reality shows, and on the faces of people in the background on the news.

At parties and in social situations, when you see someone exhibiting Extra Face, they may be hiding their true feelings and/or intent. They may be sad, lonely, or anxious. Like the extras, they know they are being observed and want to give the impression that all is well.

07: SHOULDERS PULLED BACK

It's hard to successfully execute a fake front. Quite often, the faker will overreact and go too far in the opposite direction of the emotion they want to hide. For example, keeping their normal behavior in mind, their smile will seem almost too big. They will laugh or comment a little too loudly.

Their posture might appear oddly rigid. In this case, the faker will quite often overdo it by pulling their shoulders back to push their chest out, as if to say, "Check me out. Everything is great here. Look how confident I am!" When that happens, their head tends to tilt back ever so slightly. This gives them an air of arrogance or dominance. All of these cues begin building a nonverbal picture of put-on or forced behavior.

In the same way that it's hard to keep an insincere expression on your face because there is no emotion fueling it, the realism and believability of these gestures and stances will ebb and flow as well. This makes the fake, unnatural behavior stand out as obvious, especially with those shoulders pulled back a bit too much.

08: PROTRUDING LEG

When someone at a social gathering is trying to draw the attention of others, they can't yell, "Hey! Look at me!" However, they may subconsciously exhibit body language cues or "flags" that will accomplish that goal for them. The protruding leg display is just one great example of these types of cues.

It looks similar to the way a relaxed person would put weight on their dominant leg as they lean back just a little. This movement forces the non-dominant leg forward to help the person maintain their balance.

The dominant leg in the situation we're discussing protrudes more than what would be categorized as normal. Not far enough out to make it look odd, but far enough for others to see it as: "This is my space. Check me out." Some people will exhibit similar behavior when they stand too close to a busy area or doorway, or right next to the punch bowl or gathering spot at a party.

This behavior tends to look a bit clunky, especially if the person is shy and trying to appear confident. When combined with the other cues in this illustration, the faker makes for an easy read, even at a distance.

09: EYES SCAN WHILE HEAD REMAINS STILL

This type of eye scanning behavior is not only common for the person putting on a fake front, but also the nervous person who *isn't* putting on a front. The difference being that the nervous person's eyes will dart around somewhat quickly as they check the environment for threats. The side-to-side head movement will be small and almost jerky. The shy person's eyes usually won't dart, depending on the level of anxiety they are experiencing in the situation. They tend to look down and toward the center, and they will look back up as they scan the area. What little side-to-side head movements they do make tend to be slow.

The person putting on a fake front will exhibit all of these behaviors, depending on the reason they are faking. Sometimes their eye movements will be a great deal slower than the previous two examples. The room scan may be more controlled as the brain searches for familiar faces. Their head will move just enough to be noticeable, but not deeply from side to side. This is also a common predator behavior.

10: HAND ON HIP

You've seen it a thousand times. One hand is on the hip, while the other hand holds something. This can be mistaken for a mild display of dominance. However, when seen in this situation, it stands out, similar to the way the protruding leg stands out. Think of it as a flag telling you the person is ready to, or wants to, connect.

The hand on the hip also denotes confidence when it's done the correct way. This example suggests confidence isn't high because of the hand's position. The problem is the inner rim of the hand, that part between the thumb and first finger. When that is firmly pressed against the hip forming a triangle with the elbow pointing straight out, you've got a confidence cue.

When the inner rim of the hand is just touching the hip, along with the inner side of the palm, and there is no point on the elbow, no triangle, you have a cue that denotes a relaxed or unstable confidence. Again, ready to connect, ready to talk to someone, but not a truly dominant gesture.

11: SHOULDERS SLIGHTLY SHRUGGED

In a social setting, the shy person will often exhibit a slightly forward-leaning posture with the shoulders pulled up or shrugged. This lean is not so much to look as though they have a hunched back, but it is noticeable. Some refer to this as "turtling," as the head looks like it's trying to disappear into the chest.

You will notice similar behavior when someone is surprised or experiencing fear. The shoulders quickly rise to protect the neck as the chin lowers. Once again, the ever-powerful limbic system is making sure that the neck is protected.

If you work in retail, you may want to start looking for this cue. When a thief shoplifts, they will often attempt to blend in and look smaller and harder to notice. However, shrugging and leaning forward makes them appear odd and results in them standing out, achieving the opposite effect.

When executed correctly, shrugged shoulders—combined with the other cues of shyness we're covering in this chapter—create a classic look that I teach undercover law enforcement officers to create for themselves, making it easier for them to go unnoticed and blend into a group.

12: COVERING THE CENTER OF STOMACH AREA

Shy people are often thought to be introverts, but there's a big difference between the two. The shy person doesn't like being alone. They want to connect, interact, and be with people, but are afraid to. The introvert, on the other hand, likes spending time alone and will feel drained after spending time with people.

The shy person is experiencing a form of fear. That's the reason you'll see them use barriers like the cup in the example picture. They want to put something, anything, between themselves and another person.

As the shy person's stress continues to grow, they will begin to use barriers *and* adaptors. You can get an idea of how shy a person might be by the distance the barrier they use is from their stomach area. The same thing goes for how close the under part of their forearm is to the side of their stomach. In situations like the one in the example picture, the person battling shyness will often push on the side of their stomach with the lower part of their wrist.

13: LEGS CLOSE TOGETHER

When the legs are straight and shoulder-width apart, it is referred to as "Legs Akimbo." You will see police officers, military personnel, coaches, fighters, and anyone in a dominant or alpha position using such a stance. It is one of the first nonverbal cues that communicates to people who is in charge.

The opposite posture is standing with the legs close together. It's a common display among shy people. When displaying Legs Akimbo, the person is always on balance. They look ready to take on most anything. The opposite proves true for the person standing with their legs too close together. They are often off-balance, not only physically, but also in the social situation they find themselves in as well.

They will often stand straight, leaning forward just a bit. They aren't relaxed, so they may fidget as well, but not enough to attract attention. They may sway back and forth a little or from side to side. They may lightly bounce their back on the wall, using that feeling as an adaptor or pacifier.

14: HEAD TILTED DOWNWARD

The person exhibiting a downward tilt of their head, even while in conversation, may indicate that they are experiencing sadness, loneliness, or possibly shame. With the shy person, the downward head tilt along with the slightly shrugged shoulders may not necessarily denote any of these emotions.

In a social situation, you may see the shy person with their head tilted forward and a light case of Stress Mouth creating a "Stress Smile." To make a Stress Smile, smile normally. Now, curl your lips in like you would for Stress Mouth. Ta-dah! You're the shy, nervous person in the corner making eye contact with someone passing by. This smile says, "Hello there. I'm not going to talk, but hi."

Keep in mind, this smile can be mistaken for the smile of an angry person if you do it wrong. The angry person, who isn't going to speak but is letting you know they're angry by smiling, won't nod their head as the shy person will. Their eyebrows won't be popping up for a second or so, either.

15: HAND IN POCKET

Whether at work, in the military, or at a bank meeting, the person who is lowest in the hierarchy is usually the person with their hands in their pockets. The problem with this is that most people are under the impression that keeping your hands in your pockets makes you look untrustworthy, simply because they can't see your hands. That is not actually the case. However, it is a possibility that, if observed, those in charge may get the feeling they can't trust you with an important task.

When you're in a meeting, giving a talk, or negotiating, people want to see your hands because you communicate much better when using your hands as you speak. We've talked about how your illustrators convey a level of importance that your words may not fully transmit, and people want to see those illustrators.

The thumbs play an important role in the hand-pocket relationship. When the hand is in a pocket and the thumb is displayed, that denotes a feeling of confidence. It is when the thumbs are hidden with the hands entirely in the pockets that you can count on this cue indicating shyness or being uncomfortable with the situation.

TELLTALE SIGNS OF A DISAGREEMENT

The most popular comedies always incorporate misunderstandings between characters. While one character is under the impression that a certain something is in play or will happen, another character—or maybe all of the other of the characters—are under the impression that just the opposite is true. Their actions, reactions, and body language help fuel the humor created by this misunderstanding.

These setups vary from being small enough to go unnoticed to mammoth-size setups that involve every regular actor along with several guest stars and extras. The writers know this tension builds suspense, because the viewer begins imagining how certain characters will react when receiving the misunderstood information. From Shakespeare to *Seinfeld*, misunderstandings are a go-to for humor and revealing the basics of human nature.

In real life, you may see the same intensity of stress and emotion when close friends argue. However, the close friends—depending on the argument—will tend to be more animated than the family members arguing and will often close much of the physical space between each other with no violence in mind. Meanwhile, strangers arguing may also be quite animated, depending on the situation.

The magnitude of the emotions and body language exhibited during an argument originates from a place of varied intimacy. For example, two people who don't know each other and are arguing over a parking space at the grocery store will most often argue at a distance or from inside their cars. If the windows are rolled up, the body language and facial expressions used can seem more than a bit comical to those watching at a distance. As arms begin to flail and eyes begin to widen, you may see socially unacceptable hand signs thrown out as over-the-top, exaggerated mouthing of foul language begins. As I'm sure you're aware, these displays can prove to be more than a bit humorous.

One of my favorites to observe is the argument in a bar or club parking lot between close friends who've known each other for years, especially if they've been drinking way too much and it's obvious there will be no violence. Like a sitcom, most of the time the argument stems from a misunderstanding and the body language of both parties can be quite comical. It may look and sound like you're observing a murder in progress. However, pay close attention as hands go up to slap each other but land on arms and shoulders without the full force they imply.

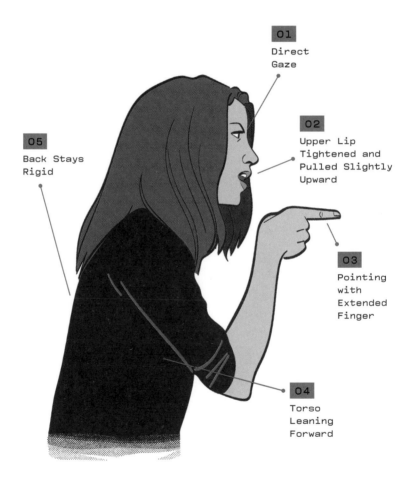

01
Direct
Gaze

02
Upper Lip
Tightened and
Pulled Slightly
Upward

05
Back Stays
Rigid

03
Pointing
with
Extended
Finger

04
Torso
Leaning
Forward

A great example of this was bought to my attention in a photo one of our neighbors took of my brother and me when we were little kids. Mitch and I were in our driveway fighting. He jumped on top of me and knocked me down. The photo shows his fist drawn back to punch me in the face, but his hand is on the back of my head protecting it from the pavement. (And no, he didn't end up punching me.)

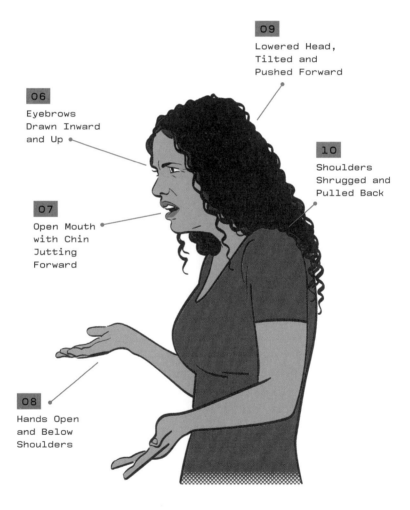

09
Lowered Head,
Tilted and
Pushed Forward

06
Eyebrows
Drawn Inward
and Up

10
Shoulders
Shrugged and
Pulled Back

07
Open Mouth
with Chin
Jutting
Forward

08
Hands Open
and Below
Shoulders

01: DIRECT GAZE

In general, there are three basic gazes: The Direct Gaze, the Social Gaze, and the Intimate Gaze. You use the Direct Gaze when meeting with someone for the first time and in business situations, times when you have permission to look at the person's eyes and forehead area.

You use the Social Gaze when you know the other person, but you don't *know* them. You're friends, but you're "work friends." With this gaze, you have permission to look at the other person's eyes and mouth area.

You use the Intimate Gaze with family members, best friends, significant others—people you're much more intimate with. These are "your people" or "your tribe," as some call it. You have permission to look at the eyes, forehead, mouth, and chest areas.

The Direct Gaze, as shown in the illustration, can instigate a fight as well as add intimidation before and during an argument. There isn't much blinking at first and the eyes are most likely squinted due to the expression of Anger.

02: UPPER LIP TIGHTENED AND PULLED SLIGHTLY UPWARD

After someone explains what happened during a tough discussion they had earlier that didn't go well, you may inevitably ask, "Well, were they mad?" If the answer is "I don't know," your second question is going to be, "Did they look mad?" The facial expression of Anger is probably the easiest to recognize, with the expression of Joy coming in at a close second.

Tighten your upper lip a little and pull it in against your top front teeth. Now curl it inward from the bottom. Now say, "That's not what I meant." You sound a bit abnormal. Now lower your voice and say it again. Similar to the person in the example picture, you look and sound about 40 percent angry. (The other 60 percent shows up when you make the entire facial expression of Anger.)

Keep in mind, the facial expression of Anger has different levels and intensities. At a lower level of anger, you'll most likely see and hear similar cues before you realize there are even smaller body language cues being exhibited as well.

03: POINTING WITH EXTENDED FINGER

If you've ever seen a commercial for a pro-wrestling event, you've seen the singular classic body language cue that tells you one of the wrestlers is angry with the other. If I were to ask you to imitate one of the wrestlers you've seen, the first thing you would do is point your finger at my face and say, "You listen to me, brrrotherrrr!" When you see that happen, no matter how far away from it you are, you know the person pointing that finger is angry.

When emotions are running high in a heated disagreement, the use of illustrators will increase dramatically. They may be used to not only emphasize specific words or phrases, but also to help create a barrier of space between the two people.

This illustrator may also be used to break into the space barrier of the other person in an attempt to dominate their "Sacred Space." Greg Hartley defines a person's Sacred Space as "the personal area around you that you control by using adaptors."

04: TORSO LEANING FORWARD

As someone arguing tries to get their point across or wants to be sure they're heard clearly, they may lean in and bend forward while at the same time leaving their feet firmly planted. The torso lean is an important cue to look for.

Here's why: When their torso leans forward, take a look at their legs. Are they slightly bent? Or are they straight and planted, so they aren't going to move? If they are straight while the torso leans forward, maybe with a hand on the hip and/or pointing a finger, as in the example picture, the chance of violence from this person at this point is fairly low.

However, during the argument, if you see the person has shifted their body weight back to their dominant leg and the non-dominant leg has moved to the front, take this as a warning sign of potential violence. The person may be preparing to lunge forward and grab you or take a swing at you. That position sets the person up to be able to make a myriad of aggressive moves that could escalate the situation.

05: BACK STAYS RIGID

Even though a person may lean their torso forward for any of the reasons we've covered, their back may remain rigid and straight. We won't go deep into pre-fight posturing, but as the limbic system switches to Freeze, Fight, or Flight mode, the muscles tense as a protective maneuver in case the body is attacked. If the muscles remained relaxed, they would be less capable of successfully sustaining blows from the other person should they lash out. Think of these tensed muscles like an exoskeleton that protects your vital organs.

Watch a boxer tempting their opponent to throw a punch as they quickly dart their head into and out of the strike zone. The boxer's back stays rigid as they lean forward to get in and out as fast as possible in hopes that his opponent will be tricked into swinging, triggering a well-timed left hook for the knockout. Keep in mind, there may be several reasons that a person leans in or leans forward before or during an argument or disagreement, but their back will remain rigid if it's true anger you're observing.

06: EYEBROWS DRAWN INWARD AND UP

When a person's face displays uncertainty and/or disbelief, their eyebrows will draw together while being pulled upward and out at the sides. Joe Navarro says, "The forehead is the billboard for our emotions." If that's true, the details of those billboard messages are displayed by the eyebrows. You may not be able to clearly see the wrinkles in someone's forehead at a distance, but you will definitely see what their eyebrows are doing.

When someone feels they are being wrongly accused or they're trying to understand why another person is angry with them, direct eye contact with eyebrows drawn inward, up, and pulled out at the sides helps create the unmistakable and classic facial expression that says "I don't understand why you think that," "What are you talking about?", etc.

When you see this cue, it will almost always be accompanied by the person shaking their head back and forth, along with squinting their eyes as if they're trying to see something more clearly.

07: OPEN MOUTH WITH CHIN JUTTING FORWARD

The chin is talked about in everything from children's stories—"Not by the hair of my chinny chin chin"—to life lessons and sage advice, such as, "You must learn to take it on the chin." People stroke their chin when thinking and throw it upward when nonverbally saying "hello" as a friend passes them in the hall or on the road.

In the picture, you can see the person's mouth is open and their chin is jutted forward, suggesting surprise and disbelief. The mouth mimics the Surprise expression and the chin juts and stays forward, suggesting, "I'm not changing my mind on this." In other words, "What? I'm surprised you think that! It was NOT me!"

The schoolyard fight exhibits many classic and quick chin juts as each opponent steps toward and away from one another. Even though the chin jut in this situation suggests aggression and/or "I'm not backing down"—or on the primal level, "See? Here's my throat. Try to grab it!"—it won't stay jutted, because if it does, there's no protection for the throat.

08: HANDS OPEN AND BELOW SHOULDERS

Open hands may be the most potent nonverbal tool a person can use. To those watching, they suggest, "I'm hiding nothing. I'm not being aggressive. Don't feel threatened by me." When the palms are pushed forward and below the shoulders, as in the picture, this is sometimes referred to as "Mercy Hands." They say to the other person, "Please believe me. Have mercy!" That's exactly what this person's hands are transmitting nonverbally: "Don't be threatened by me. Whatever it is, I didn't do it. Believe me, it wasn't me!"

If the hands were doing the same thing but above the shoulders, the message would be similar but more along the lines of "I don't know" or "I'm not sure." It would be unnatural for them to be above the shoulders when conveying the "It wasn't me, I didn't do it" message, and it would suggest there's more to the story. Like all the nonverbal cues we've discussed, it wouldn't mean for sure that the person was lying. However, it would give you cause to keep asking questions about whatever subject they are denying.

09: LOWERED HEAD, TILTED AND PUSHED FORWARD

The head tilted to the side suggests the person's attention is focused on and is trying to understand what the other person is doing or saying. This is normal when someone is being accused, especially when it's a surprise, as in the example picture. With the head pushed forward, the neck is unprotected. It's the brain saying, "Look, I'm vulnerable. I'm not on the counterattack. I don't need to be. I didn't do anything."

When the head is lowered, it shows there is no attempt to dominate the situation. In a way, it's offering an act of submission to the accuser. If a friend of yours says, "I know you took all the money out of my wallet" and you're not expecting it, you won't start yelling and trying to dominate the situation. You will most likely display nonverbal cues that say, "What? I have no idea what you're talking about." After your head recoils and your eyebrows pull inward, up, and out, the head tilted and pushed forward will most likely be your brain's next move.

10: SHOULDERS SHRUGGED AND PULLED BACK

When the limbic system triggers the Freeze, Fight, or Flight mode, it begins protecting you as other parts of the brain quickly gather information about the unfolding situation. The last thing it wants to do is expose your chest area, because that's where your heart and lungs are.

When you see a person with their shoulders shrugged and pulled back, like in the example picture, their chest is exposed. This, along with the other nonverbal cues we've looked at, tells us this person isn't worried about violence. They are more concerned with letting the other person know they have come to an incorrect conclusion about the accusation against them.

The shoulder shrug is an almost universal nonverbal cue that says, "I don't know," "I don't understand," "I'm not sure," and/or "I'm confused about what just happened." If the person is pretending that they don't understand, the shoulder shrug lasts around a half second or less. A real shrug can last from one second to a second and a half, and sometimes it can even last as long as two or three seconds.

HOW TO FEEL PHYSICALLY ASSURED IN DIFFICULT SITUATIONS

In this chapter, we learned you can gather an incredible amount of information about someone and how they may be feeling just by observing their body language as they stand around at a social gathering. By that same token, we can transmit what we want others to think about us by simply adjusting our own body language. For example, after reading this chapter, you have all the information you need to look and feel like the most confident person in every social situation you find yourself in. So, let's focus on the five most important cues we went over, in no specific order.

1. **SMILE.** The easiest and most potent nonverbal cue you can exhibit is a smile. Nothing too big or unnatural for the situation, but a smile you've practiced in the bathroom mirror. One that's small, pleasant, and relaxed.

2. **LEGS AKIMBO.** Don't go overboard with this one. When standing, make sure your legs are about shoulder-width apart. Don't sway back and forth if you're a swayer.

3. **SHOULDERS PULLED BACK.** When you look like you're not worried or guarded, you're much more approachable. This cue will make you feel confident as well.

4. **POSTURE.** Keeping your back straight is important. People can see you slouching from across the street.

5. **CHIN UP.** You've heard people say, "Keep your chin up." That's because it makes you look and feel confident. Make sure it isn't up so high that it makes you look arrogant. There's a fine line there.

There you have it. The top five body language cues that will make you look and feel confident. Go out and use them!

FOUR:

DECODING THE HIDDEN MESSAGES OF DATING

THE IMPORTANCE OF understanding body language in the dating scene cannot be understated. Did your date this weekend turn out to be the romantic occasion you thought it would be? Or were you counting the seconds until it was over? In this chapter, we will dive into the hidden messages of dating, providing you with valuable signs that you were most likely not aware of, or thought to look for.

In high school, a friend of mine asked a classmate out on a date. That Friday night, they went to Big Ed's Pizza and saw a movie. He called the next morning with awesome news. "We had a blast. She's kind of shy and she didn't eat much, but I had her laughing during the whole movie. It couldn't have gone better!"

Later, I got another call from the best friend of the girl my friend went out with. "What's up with your buddy?" she asked. "What do you mean?" "Lisa told me she and Bill went to Big Ed's and he would not stop talking. She couldn't get a word in edgewise. And he ate almost all of the pizza. Then he talked through the entire movie!"

Here's a perfect example of two people misunderstanding each other's body language and behavior. He liked her, but he was so nervous he couldn't shut up. She liked him at first, but she thought he wasn't interested because he talked so much and wouldn't listen when she tried to talk. Both had good intentions. However, misreading each other's body language cost them what could have been an awesome date. (They tried again in college, got married, and now have two little girls. True story.)

HOW TO READ WHEN THINGS ARE GOING WELL

There are many nonverbal ways that humans broadcast their interest in one another. For example, what's the first thing you would do if I asked you to show the person sitting across the table that you're attracted to them? I've got $1000 that says you'd smile.

If that person across the table finds you attractive or if they are the least bit intrigued, they are going to show you a few cues to let you know how they feel. A woman will most likely pull her hair behind one ear and make sure the side of her neck is visible. You'll probably get a good look at her wrists as well. Something else you might see is her nostrils flaring just a little bit. Her brain is trying to locate some of your pheromones in the air to get an idea of what your scent is like.

Your eyebrows will most likely go up as you nonverbally indicate you'd like a response of some sort from her. Your pupils will also dilate as you try to take in as much of her visually as you can, and you're going to stare a little bit. Not that creepy stare of stalkers in the movies and TV shows, but the long gaze executed just right that lets her know you're very interested in her. She's going to gaze right back at you the very same way, although she may break eye contact before you.

Her lips may begin to look a bit red as the blood flows to her cheeks, lips, and brow. You'll probably take in a deep breath before you even realize you're doing it. Your nostrils will flare a little, because your brain is now looking for her pheromones to give you an idea of her scent.

During this time, you should start paying attention to the number of breaths she is taking. Is her breathing speeding up or slowing down? If she's attracted to you, her breaths per minute will increase and you will begin to notice a few deeper breaths as well. Her smile will still be there, but it will be smaller. Then it will go back and forth from smaller, to a bit larger, to a bit smaller, to a bit larger. This is good. She's thinking.

Now see if she has moved her hands or arms so that they are positioned similarly to yours. If she has, that's a great sign. If she hasn't? Then you can casually move your hands, then your arms, into similar positions as hers. Here's where you're going to learn how interested she really is. After a couple of minutes, if she positions her hands and arms so they are similar to yours, you can feel confident things from this point on are going to go very well. You've seen the nonverbals that show you her brain is reacting to you and wants to get to know you better. Now, let's get into some details . . .

01 Head Tilted Exposing Neck

02 Blink Rate Slows

03 Bedroom Eyes

04 Flushed Cheeks

05 Steady Eye Gazing

06 Leaning Forward

07 Space Between Fingers

08 Shoulder Down and Forward

09 Lowered Tone of Voice

10 Leg Jiggling Under Table

01: HEAD TILTED EXPOSING NECK

In this chapter, we will dive into the hidden messages of dating, providing you with valuable signs you most likely were previously not aware of to look for.

The tilted head exposing the neck is one of the first nonverbal cues you'll notice when a woman is attracted to someone. As we talk about the head tilt in a dating situation, it's important to note that humans secrete pheromones to help attract a mate. One of the common ways the body releases pheromones is through sweating. By exposing her neck, not only is she subconsciously saying she is vulnerable, but she is also saying, "Check out these pheromones!" The head and neck are prone to heating up and lightly sweating as the woman becomes aroused.

When the person the woman finds attractive is attracted to her, that person will also begin secreting more pheromones than usual. When thinking of pheromones, think of them almost like chemical messengers relaying the intentions of one aroused person to another. There's much more going on with pheromones and how we react to them than can be covered here, but it's important you get the basics so you'll at least be familiar with how they fit into understanding human behavior.

02: BLINK RATE SLOWS

When someone asks you to look at something, to focus on it because they have a question about it, your blink rate slows. Not a great deal, but it is noticeable. When you're watching a movie and someone is sneaking up behind the star of the movie with a knife, your blink rate slows as well.

Why does this happen? When excited, your brain wants to see as much of whatever it is you're looking at as it possibly can. The same goes for when you're attracted to someone. Your brain says, "Hang on a second. This person appeals to me in every way. I want a really good look at them. There are some things I'd like to know."

In the example picture, the woman isn't just looking at her date; she's taking in every move they make, everything they're wearing, and everything they say, because her brain has become aroused. At the same time, her brain is sifting through that information, trying to verify what she is feeling and making sure the potential mate is not a threat.

03: BEDROOM EYES

When it comes to dating and romance, the eyes are infamous. Crooners sing about them in love songs, poets write about them in sonnets, and they are often the most mysterious highlight of an artist's painting.

When you hear the term "Bedroom Eyes," it's being used in a specific context, usually a sexual context. It refers to a specific look some women try to recreate with makeup to help mimic the look of a woman's eyes when she is sexually aroused. When the eyes are nearly half closed or heavy lidded and the pupils are also dilated, *that* is Bedroom Eyes. That is what you're seeing in the example.

Research tells us that when the same makeup styling that creates Bedroom Eyes for women is instead used on a man, the result looks so odd and out of character for what men's eyes look like during sexual arousal that women find this very unattractive and somewhat scary. If you're trying to decide if your date finds you attractive or not, take a closer look at their eyes.

04: FLUSHED CHEEKS

Cartoonists and digital artists are some of the best readers of body language and nonverbal cues on the planet. Why are they so good at translating human behavior into drawings? Because when they're not drawing, they're watching the way people behave in every situation you can possibly imagine. They are literally studying the body language of everyday people. They're experts.

For example, when you're watching a cartoon and you see the girl mouse meet the boy mouse for the first time, there are several things you can tell me right now that are about to happen. The first thing she's going to do is start batting her eyes. After that? She'll clasp her fingers together and push her wrists and palms outward and down a little bit. And after that? Her head will tilt to the side. Last but not least, her cheeks will blush.

Blushing cheeks denote embarrassment and sometimes anger. They can also indicate sexual arousal and attraction. When you see this on your date's face and cheeks, things are going really well.

05: STEADY EYE GAZING

A predator, human or animal, will keep its eyes on its prey no matter what the prey does or where it goes. It will follow and, when the time is right, attack. On the other hand, you have the non-predator human. On a date—and this goes for everyone—if the woman finds her date attractive, she'll keep a steady eye on them. Not because she thinks they're going to attack her, but because her brain wants to keep taking in as much information about the potential mate as it possibly can. Is the subject she's talking about interesting to him? Is the potential mate in a good mood?

The date will be looking at her, too. He'll be thinking the same things. Their eyes will meet and their brains will tell them, "This is good. You're connecting with this person. Keep doing it." Keep in mind, if the steady eye gazing behavior starts too early by either participant, it's going to give the other a creepy feeling. It's one of those things you have to ease into naturally.

06: LEANING FORWARD

There are many ways humans show they are attracted to or are interested in another person, especially in a dating scenario. You'll likely see and hear some if not all of the things we've already discussed, and there are a few others that aren't as noticeable that you'll probably see as the date progresses. For example, the leaning forward we see in the picture. Some might say, "Ah, he's using the table as a barrier by leaning toward it like that." You can understand why they may say that, but let's look closer.

If he wanted to distance himself from his date, he would just sit straight up with both hands and arms on the table acting as barriers as well. By doing that, he would be adding even more space between them. However, when he leans forward, he's closing the distance between himself and the other person. Subconsciously, he's trying to get as close to the potential partner as he can. Notice his head is pushed forward just a bit as well. The date has his complete attention.

07: SPACE BETWEEN FINGERS

When a person is angry, worried, or anxious, there are several hand cues they may exhibit. As their anger grows, a person will most likely clinch their dominant hand into a fist, as though they are preparing to throw a punch. The worried and/or anxious person will exhibit the classic hand-wringing cues, rubbing their hands together or rubbing the right hand's palm with the left hand's thumb. They may put one, two, three, or all four fingers and thumb in one hand and squeeze them.

At the other end of the spectrum, when someone is relaxed, their hands are prone to relax, as in the picture. Even though they are holding a cup of coffee, there is plenty of space between the fingers. When you see this, it suggests that the person is not worried or stressed. When the space goes away, something has changed, signifying there's an issue. Sometimes it goes away slowly and sometimes it goes away quickly, depending on the situation. Look for this cue not only on dates, but in meetings as well.

08: SHOULDER DOWN AND FORWARD

For the same reasons we discussed "leaning forward" previously, this nonverbal cue is an important one. The difference in the two is this: He's so interested in his date that he doesn't realize he's moving even closer by pushing his shoulder forward. At the same time, this positions his body at an angle to his potential partner's. This is good for his date because the other person's brain will see he isn't squaring off with them as he continues trying to get closer and his movement will be seen as less of a threat.

In situations where tension and tempers are running high, at first you will see the two people arguing stand with their shoulders and legs squared off to each other, like the gunfighters in old movies. It's an aggressive stance. That's why, when you meet someone for the first time, it's good to shake hands and then sidestep just a little and slightly angle your body position versus theirs. The other person's brain will relax a bit knowing that your body language says, "I'm a friend. I like you."

09: LOWERED TONE OF VOICE

Voice tone plays an important role when persuading others to do what you want them to do. If a person's voice is high-pitched, shrill, and loud, that lets others know something's wrong. If their voice is in a normal range and isn't at an increased volume, others immediately get the feeling that everything is fine. What about your tone of voice on a date? We know that, by lowering your voice tone and volume, two things will happen:

1. The other person will come a little closer to try and hear you better. They may lean in a bit or even scoot their chair closer.

2. The lowered voice tone will make the other person's brain release oxytocin.

Oxytocin is the bonding chemical that floods a new mother's brain when she holds her baby for the first time. It's the tone Barry White uses in his love songs. When you lower your voice tone, it indicates you are trying to create a bond with the other person. However, if you lower it too much, it sounds creepy.

10: LEG JIGGLING UNDER TABLE

Most people are under the impression that a jiggling leg under the table is bad news, especially on a date. It's believed that the person jiggling their leg is lying, nervous, scared, and/or a myriad of other things. It *can* mean all of those things. However, you must take the behaviors you're seeing and put them in context with what's happening in that specific situation in real time.

If we look at the other behaviors exhibited in the example picture, we can feel confident with deciding he's in no way a threat. The jiggling leg was most likely triggered by his excitement at being on a first date

On the other hand, if his leg wasn't jiggling and his date asked him a question about his history or background—for example, "Have you ever been in trouble with the law?"—and his leg started jiggling, then there is cause to ask more questions around that subject. By the same token, if his leg *was* jiggling and after that question it stopped? His date *better* ask more questions about that subject.

HOW TO USE POSITIVE
BODY LANGUAGE ON A DATE

A date is an organic group of presentations, especially a first date. Both participants put their best qualities on display during their time together. Person A will sit up a little straighter and speak with a stronger, lower voice. Person B will often try to look impressed by what Person A says or does. Whatever one presents, the other will find fascinating. As long as this psychological ping-pong game remains in motion, things will go well.

As the dating ritual continues, participants can do things to look and feel more confident. For many, the less they move, the more mature and in control they appear. For others, the more they keep eye contact and look relaxed, the more in control they appear. When questions arise, sometimes it's hard not to just blurt something out. To give the impression every word in the question is important, the one answering should pause just for half a moment before answering. Doing so gives the impression that the question has been given some thought. It may not sound like a big deal, but it's huge.

The participants shouldn't be afraid to invade the other's space. I don't mean one should just reach out and put their hands on the other. Just walk a little closer to the other person. There should be no fear of leaning toward the other a little bit when sitting together if it's a movie date, when standing together if it's a social engagement, or when waiting to cross the street together. If things are going well, there will be no problem at all with this little bit of space-invading.

CHECK, PLEASE! HOW TO KNOW WHEN YOUR DATE ISN'T GOING WELL

We all have at least one funny story about being on a date that didn't go well. Maybe you knew it was doomed after the first five minutes. Maybe you knew ten minutes after you got to the restaurant. Or maybe you watched it slowly unravel right in the middle of your entrée. Whatever the timeline, there are probably a few cues you didn't realize you were seeing that would have told you things were heading south fast. Let's go over a few of the more common tells you may have missed that will let you know when things are going poorly.

At first, you may have noticed an uncomfortable smile but you didn't think much of it. You know the one. It was a little too big, there were no teeth showing, and the eyes were "dead." It stayed that way for a few seconds, but you kept watching. Just before it went away, you saw the bottom lip curl inward just a little, followed by the upper lip curling the same way. Then you saw, ever so quickly, just for a fleeting moment, the lips pursing to one side. Oh no . . . These were all telltale signs letting you know that your date was crashing on takeoff.

Next, you may have noticed that eye contact was sparse. It was there, but it didn't connect for long at all. When it did, it was uncomfortable. At this point, both hands were probably under the table. Then again, maybe just one was under while the other was clumsily fidgeting with a wine glass or a fork. You kept asking great questions, but the answers always came back in short sentences with the head nodding a bit too long, and those lips kept doing that curling-and-pursing-to-the-side thing. Then you noticed there were no questions coming back your way, so you began feeling like an interrogator.

There were a few long pauses between your questions, and your date's hands were both on the table. One was on top of the other and there was no space at all between their fingers. Then, their posture slowly turned into a semi-slouch, beginning to resemble Quasimodo's posture as he headed for the stairs of the bell tower. Even though you tried your best to remain engaged, your date kept checking the room and slyly trying to get a look at what was going on behind you.

I'll bet it wasn't long after that when your date said something like, "Excuse me, I need to find the restroom." After ten minutes or so, you probably thought to yourself, "Hmmm . . . Maybe the restroom is at that gas station across the street." Then you spotted your date across the room on the way back to your table as they put their phone away. This is probably when you began to panic as it dawned on you that this date had not only crashed, but it had been burning on the runway for the last 30 minutes.

01 Single Raised Eyebrow

02 Slouched Posture

03 Thumb and Forefinger Slightly Pressed Against Face

04 One Side of Upper Lip Slightly Raised

05 Arm Creating Barrier

06 Eyelids Closed for Too Long

07 Self-Grooming or Preening

08 Yawning

09 Rigid Posture

10 Feet Pointed Toward the Door

01: SINGLE RAISED EYEBROW

Eyebrows cue you in on a myriad of emotions. When dating, you want to see both eyebrows of the other person raising to let you know they're listening and engaged. When you tell that story about the time your dog ran away, you'll be looking for the eyebrows to be pulled together toward the middle to show your date is identifying with you emotionally.

When you tell that story about the time you won $100 in the lottery, you'll be hoping to see their eyebrows way up while they smile. As you talk back and forth, you can get a fairly good read on how things are going by the amount of, and the different kinds of, eyebrow movement you see.

In this example, we see the one thing you don't want to see: the head tilted to one side while one eyebrow is pulled upward and the other eyebrow is pulled slightly downward. This indicates the person is feeling doubt and/or uncertainty about the other person or the subject being discussed.

02: SLOUCHED POSTURE

When you see comfort between two people on a date, quite often you'll notice mirroring. For example, if one person is leaning to the right, the other will lean that way as well. If one puts both elbows on the table out in front, it won't be long before the other mimics that same behavior.

Not only will you see mirroring in smaller cues, you'll see them writ large in the legs and torso. The torso plays an important role here as it is shaped by the person's posture. When we are paying close attention, our posture will be fairly straight and sometimes quite rigid. Posture can indicate respect as well as disdain.

In the example, we see a slouched posture that denotes boredom, and it's probably an unconscious show of disrespect. If the date were going well and the woman displayed this posture, it would be likely that the man would be displaying the same or a similar posture. Her slouching, combined with everything else her body language is screaming at us, lets us know this date is almost over.

03: THUMB AND FOREFINGER SLIGHTLY PRESSED AGAINST FACE

Quite often, you will see this behavior without realizing it. It's triggered by anything from stress to excitement, by something good or something bad. One thing is for sure when you see it: Something's up.

In the picture, we see the woman with her thumb and index finger pushing against her cheek and temple. This suggests she's stressed from listening to and being with someone she is not the least bit attracted to. As she tries to remain patient, you may observe other cues of her impatience or unease as well.

Joe Navarro calls this specific behavior "Facial Denting." It describes what it looks like when someone is pushing in on the side of their face or mouth with a finger, or even a pen or a pencil. As with all pacification cues, Facial Denting helps relieve the built-up tension and/or stress caused by everything from watching a sporting event to watching your child perform for the first time in a school play. You may also see it when someone is in deep thought or making an important decision.

04: ONE SIDE OF UPPER LIP SLIGHTLY RAISED

Although Charles Darwin first suggested in the late 1800s that facial expressions of emotion are the same (universal) everywhere in the world, it was Paul Ekman and his team of scientists in the late 1960s and early 1970s who proved that there were at least seven universal expressions that exist everywhere around the world:

1. **ANGER**

2. **HAPPINESS**

3. **SADNESS**

4. **DISGUST**

5. **FEAR**

6. **SURPRISE**

7. **CONTEMPT**

Each expression uses specific facial muscles. The expression we see on the woman's face in the picture is Contempt. The upper lip pulled up on one side is the telltale sign. Sometimes it can be seen by everyone in the room, and sometimes it's so subtle and it comes and goes so quickly that you would need a magnifying glass and a slow-motion camera to catch it. If you see this facial expression on your date, you might as well ask for the check. The date's been over for a while and you just found out.

05: ARM CREATING BARRIER

I got a call from a group of venture capitalists who told me they had invested $2.2 million in a startup and things just didn't seem right. They asked me to talk to the CEO and see whether I felt they should be concerned. I met with the CEO in an attorney's office. When I began asking what was happening with the investors' money, he took a drink of coffee and put the cup on the table between us. As we continued to talk for a little over an hour, he put a pen and pad of paper between us.

By the time the meeting was over, he had put one of those big conference phones, his phone, and his watch on the table between us. Why would he exhibit such bizarre behavior? He was trying to separate himself from me. He was uncomfortable because I was asking valid questions he couldn't answer. In the example picture, we see the woman behaving similarly. She's using her arm as a barrier to help put space between her and her horrifically boring date.

06: EYELIDS CLOSED FOR TOO LONG

When presented with something we find offensive, gross, or unpleasant, we may instinctively close our eyes to block out what we're seeing. Sometimes we'll even put our hands up and cover our eyes to put more distance between us and the object of our disgust. We may also do that when given bad news. This behavior is referred to as—you guessed it—Eye Blocking. That's what's happening in the example picture. The guy is keeping his eyes closed a little too long when blinking because he doesn't like his date. Not even a little bit.

In fact, people who have been blind their entire lives will put up their hands to block their eyes when given bad news or told a graphic joke. Some will even block them when they hear a description of a vulgar scene or situation. Researchers have no idea why this behavior is so universal. It isn't a learned behavior, since they for sure haven't seen anyone doing it. This is one of those cases where the nature versus nurture discussion and human behavior get really interesting.

07: SELF-GROOMING OR PREENING

When things are going well, there's nothing wrong with self-grooming or preening. If you see the person you're meeting with straighten their tie or brush off their dress or pants when you enter the room, this can be taken as a sign that they respect and/or admire you. It lets you know they are making themselves as presentable as possible and trying to make the best impression.

However, there are times when self-grooming and preening are not good. If you're in court standing in front of a judge and she asks, "How do you plead?" and you answer, "Not guilty" while pulling a hair off the sleeve of your shirt or brushing something off of your shoulder, you just let her know you have no respect whatsoever for her, the robes, or the court.

In this example, we see the man pulling or brushing lint from his lapel while at the same time answering his date's question. He's not looking at his date. Not only does this indicate disrespect, it flaunts that disrespect.

08: YAWNING

Most people are under the impression that yawning indicates a singular, specific meaning: that the person is sleepy or tired. There are times when that *is* the proper connotation. However, it is not true in every situation.

A yawn accomplishes several tasks for the human body. For example, if you find yourself in a situation where tension and/or stress is beginning to build, you may yawn unexpectedly. As your muscles tighten and your body becomes a little stiff, your brain may decide you need a shot of oxygen and it will trigger a yawn. Sometimes, when children get a little overheated, they will yawn because that rush of air through the mouth, down the throat, and into the lungs helps lower their body's temperature.

In this example, the man indicates his disinterest in what his date is talking about by yawning. He's not doing it on purpose. He's just becoming bored from sitting and not moving. If you were asked to sit and listen to a podcast about a subject you had no interest in whatsoever, after seven to nine minutes, you're going to yawn.

09: RIGID POSTURE

A rigid posture can indicate many things. If you're on a roller coaster, your posture will become extremely rigid during the ride up to that first drop. That's normal. You can't help it. You're bracing yourself because your limbic system is on fire. Likewise, if you were told someone just ran up and grabbed your mother's purse, your posture would become rigid as your anger climbed from 0 to 100 in a few short seconds.

Quite often, when we find ourselves in a stressful social situation, the muscles in our back and neck will begin to tighten. This happens while our brain attempts to maintain an air of normality while running scenarios of the quickest ways to bring the predicament to a close. When we put together all the nonverbal cues we've seen in this situation, it becomes obvious he's not into this date at all. Theoretically, if the date was going well, his posture should mimic hers or hers should mimic his. That's not happening here, and it's probably a sign that this match isn't meant to be.

10: FEET POINTED TOWARD THE DOOR

One of the many things Navy SEALs are taught about human behavior is how to spot the leader of a group by looking at the feet of those in the group. You can do this, too, by taking note of which person most of the feet in the group are pointed towards. *That* person is the focus of the group. That's who they are interested in and who they will listen to. That person is most likely the leader or alpha of the group. A person's feet point toward who or what they are interested in.

If you're at a party and a guy is talking to you and your best friend with his feet pointed toward you and not her? You can bet he's more interested in you. If his feet are pointed toward the door? He wants to, or is desiring to, leave soon. In the example picture, the woman's feet are pointed at the door, not at her date. For her, the date is over and she wants to leave.

HOW TO CHANGE YOUR BODY LANGUAGE TO IMPROVE THE DATE

Turning a dating situation from bad to good isn't as tough as you might think. I know because I train new interrogators how to persuade suspects they're interrogating to like them. Why would they want to do that?

Think about this: What four words can a suspect say to end the interrogation? You guessed it. "I want a lawyer." For that reason, you must persuade the suspect to like you or at least feel comfortable with you, so they'll want to stay. You want their brain to fire off oxytocin, serotonin, and dopamine. Those are the bonding chemicals known as the "Happy Hormones." Here's how you can do it, using what you've learned so far. Take your time going through these steps.

IN SCENARIO 1, YOU'RE THE WOMAN:

→   When your date is talking, take a semi-deep breath and slowly begin to smile that slow and tiny smile we talked about earlier. When you smile, the mirror neurons of your date's brain will fire and they'll smile back. Slowly tilt your head to the side a bit and turn on those Bedroom Eyes we talked about. Pull your hair back behind your ear, even if you have short hair. Look down at the table and slowly back up at them. You'll know this is working when you see their eyebrows go up. This may take a few minutes, but trust me. I've seen it work a thousand times.

IN SCENARIO 2, YOU'RE THE MAN:

→ When your date is talking, tilt your head forward a little and make eye contact as you load that slow and tiny smile. Your date's mirror neurons will fire, so they'll smile a little. Nod your head a bit, like you're listening. Try not to move much. Let them see that they have your complete attention. When it's your turn to talk, lower your voice tone just enough to be noticeable. When your date's eyebrows go up, or if they're doing the things in Scenario 1, you've officially turned things around.

FIVE:

TRANSLATING BODY LANGUAGE IN A JOB INTERVIEW

JOB INTERVIEWS ARE INFAMOUS FOR rattling nerves and creating stressful situations. That's why it's of the utmost importance to understand body language and nonverbal behavior, not just from the interviewer's perspective but from the interviewee's perspective as well, because the chances of both participants misunderstanding the body language of the other are extremely high.

For example, ten minutes into the interview, the interviewee may let out a big breath with a sigh. The interviewer notices this and thinks, "This person seems bored. How disrespectful!"

However, in reality, the interviewee is finally relaxing and feeling good about how things are going and unconsciously lets out a sigh of relief. Then the candidate notices a frown popping up and disappearing quickly from the interviewer's face and thinks, "Oh no! They don't like me! This *isn't* going well!" Their face shows a slight expression of fear as they adjust in their seat to help pacify themselves, and keep their nerves calm.

The interviewer sees this and believes it to be insecurity about the topic they are currently focusing on. The interviewer thinks, "Okay . . . There it is. This candidate has no idea how to put together a TPS report. I'll cut this short and get on to the next interview." The next thing you know, the interviewee is walking to their car asking themselves, "What happened? Everything was going great, then it just turned completely around. I knew I shouldn't have worn this jacket . . ." The interview is over. The candidate doesn't get the job. And neither person has any idea what really happened.

HOW TO KNOW WHEN A JOB INTERVIEW IS GOING WELL

There's nothing like going to a job interview and crushing it. But have you ever been to one that you thought went horribly wrong, yet you got the job? Why does *that* happen? It happens because the nonverbal cues that tell us all is well slip right by us. The key to understanding body language in a job interview situation is paying attention from the very beginning of the meeting. This is when the interviewer is in the most neutral setting. Any variation from these behaviors will stick out.

When the interviewer asks you the first question, look for their head to tilt to one side just a bit. How about their ears? Is one turned just a touch toward you? Are they nodding a little every few sentences or so? What about their eyebrows? Are they in the up position? If you see all of these cues, that's good. They are telling you they're listening, paying attention, and wanting to know more. Not long from now, those eyebrows will pull together and up in the middle. The interviewer is thinking. This is good, but only if their head remains tilted. It's going to straighten up in a minute or two, but you want that initial conversational answer to be received with a wide-open set of nonverbals that tell you all is well.

To test the waters a little bit here, you're going to want to smile. Not a big smile, but a slow and tiny smile. The one that begins very tiny and gradually grows to small. Don't smile a big smile. It will look odd and out of place. You want it to start slow, so when their mirror neurons fire off, she'll mirror a small smile. This will trigger a positive emotion for the interviewer, and they will feel good about you and have no idea why. (This is an old interrogation trick.)

When things are going well, you may see them lean forward a bit. They want to move closer because they're beginning to like you. If you're close enough, you may see their pupils dilate. This happens when we see something we find interesting or when we find something or someone we're attracted to. They see you as an asset to the company, so they find you very interesting. Hopefully, they're going to cross their arms and maybe even touch their face. It can't get any better than this. These cues combined let you know that they've got some heavy inner dialogue going on. The interviewer is still listening, but they're thinking of some questions that aren't on their list, because they see potential here.

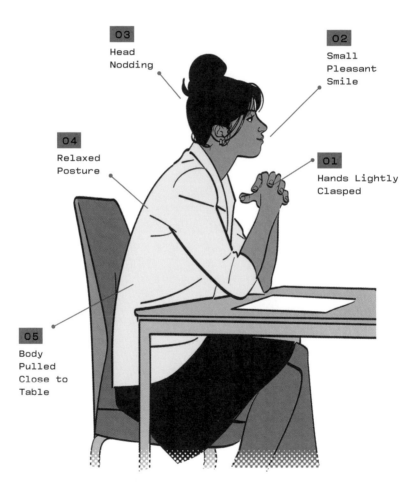

03 Head Nodding

02 Small Pleasant Smile

04 Relaxed Posture

01 Hands Lightly Clasped

05 Body Pulled Close to Table

Can you see their feet? Which way are they pointing? If they're pointed at you, that indicates you've got their full attention. Our feet point toward the person or place we are concerned with or interested in. As their arms uncross, if they go to the desk and they prop up on their elbows just a bit with their hands clasped in front of them, the interviewer most likely has one question left and it's a good one. Hopefully, it will be "So, when can you start?"

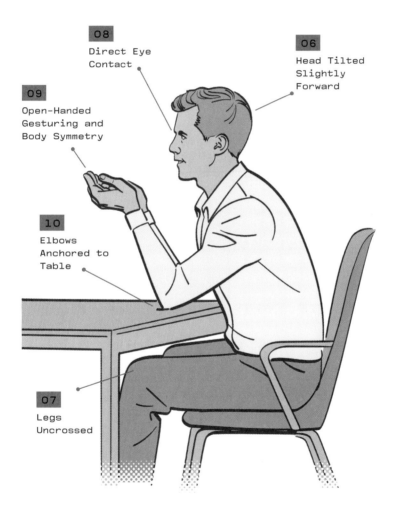

08
Direct Eye Contact

06
Head Tilted Slightly Forward

09
Open-Handed Gesturing and Body Symmetry

10
Elbows Anchored to Table

07
Legs Uncrossed

01: HANDS LIGHTLY CLASPED

We hear so much about hands when learning about interpersonal communication due to the important role they play. Hands show us how emphatic or relaxed a person's illustrators are. They show us a variety of adaptors, cluing us in on the stress level and mindset of the person we're observing. Hands can even be used as barriers.

The example picture shows us what might be mistaken for a barrier, as it does in fact look similar to someone trying to distance themselves. However, there are a few things that let you know this person is showing interest, not stress or a need to create distance between themselves and the other person.

The most important thing is the lightly clasped hands. There is plenty of space between the fingers, suggesting that the person is relaxed. It also shows us a relaxed form of steepling that suggests this person is confident and in charge. Even though the arms and lightly clasped hands look like barriers, the hands are angled back toward the interviewer and under the chin. This suggests focused interest on the interviewee.

02: SMALL PLEASANT SMILE

A big smile from the job interviewer is a good sign if, and only if, it doesn't stay for the entire interview. If it stays the whole time, something is wrong with that person mentally or they know you won't be back and they're being nice. You won't see that scenario often, but when you do, you might as well thank them for their time and leave.

You do want to see the big smile when you first meet and then again when you're leaving. The rest of the time you want to see a small but pleasant smile, nothing overbearing or "too much." That smile will let you know they're engaged, listening, and interested in you.

If that smile goes away for a few minutes every now and then, that's actually good. They're focusing on you and what you've said at that point. When they've taken in that information and/or made a decision about it, the small pleasant smile will return. By the same token, you want to wear a small and pleasant smile throughout the meeting as well.

03: HEAD NODDING

One of the telltale signs of a good listener is head nodding. It lets us know the listener is taking everything in. When their head is nodding along with the small and pleasant smile we just talked about, you've got a powerful combination of nonverbal cues that let you know you're in charge right now.

Also, when you see their head nodding, nod your head just a bit. That may be the most natural mirroring situation you'll ever find yourself in. When you're both nodding, you're agreeing. This is a potent tool when creating a relationship with a possible employer. Plus, it's going to give you a little more time to talk, since it helps keep them in listening mode.

Don't nod the whole time. Nod almost as if your nod is helping power their nod and it's giving them energy to keep nodding. You'll have to do it two or three times to get the timing right. When you do, you'll be surprised at how open they are for the rest of the interview.

04: RELAXED POSTURE

When two friends are seated at a table in a coffee shop, you'll see relaxed postures. They will be leaning inward with their upper torsos lowered slightly and their elbows and/or forearms on the table. They're displaying comfort, whereas slouching displays discomfort and boredom.

They're taking turns listening and talking. That's the look you want to see from the other side of the table during your job interview. You may feel this posture is a dismissive behavior. Maybe it's the interviewer's way of showing they really don't care about what you're talking about. Nope. Don't confuse this relaxed posture with slouching. You'll see exactly what I'm talking about with the interviewer in the example picture.

When the posture is slouched, everything else will look wilted as well. The interviewer will be bent to one side or have their hands in their lap, with shoulders down, head tilted back, and pushing the chin forward. The relaxed posture looks and feels pleasant, with visible hands and that small, pleasant smile we talked about earlier.

05: BODY PULLED CLOSE TO TABLE

We talked about the use of barriers as we saw President Clinton leaning so close to the podium that he could almost push it over with his stomach. We're seeing something similar in the example picture. However, the interviewer isn't using the table as a barrier. This is a good sign.

When you're being interviewed and the interviewer scoots as close to the table as they can get while still remaining relaxed, they are very interested in you and in what you have been saying. The move won't happen all at once. You'll see their arms move to the top of the table. As you keep talking, you'll see them lean in a bit. To get more comfortable, they're going to scoot little by little, closer and closer to you. The only thing separating them from you is the table.

When you notice this, you're going to think, "I should move closer to them." Don't. You're doing fine. Let them do the moving. If you lean in, they may realize you're moving toward them and things could take a turn for the awkward.

06: HEAD TILTED SLIGHTLY FORWARD

The proper head tilt can denote anything from physical attraction to showing you're ready to receive an answer to your question. In an interview, you may notice the interviewer's head tilt back just a bit as they ask a question. After that, their head may tilt to the side a little. That's the cue that lets you know they're ready and waiting for your answer. It's totally normal. However, if you tilt your head back when you answer, you're going to resemble an arrogant know-it-all who's talking down to the interviewer.

As you answer, hopefully you'll see the interviewer's head go from tilting back to a light tilt to one side. When you see that, you've got her undivided attention. Then we have the forward tilt. The forward tilt we see in the example lets us know that the interviewee is giving information they feel is important. There are times when the forward tilt indicates aggression or even browbeating, but when it's executed smoothly, it helps capture and keep the attention of the person receiving the information.

07: LEGS UNCROSSED

When the interviewee has uncrossed legs with both feet flat on the floor, not only does this help keep their posture straight, it adds to the symmetry they're creating with their elbow anchoring and their use of illustrators. It also helps give the impression of stability, focus, and paying attention.

When training people for job interviewing, the first thing I have them do is sit down as if we're in the middle of an interview and show me what they believe the interviewee should look like. I have them go through everything, from the way they breathe to the way they leave. I also have them sit across the table from me as if I'm the interviewer. Then I have them sit in a chair or on a couch and have them do the same thing.

Sometimes the interviewer will tell you to relax and they'll say, "Let's just talk for a bit." When that happens, do just that. You can cross your legs and relax, but it's still important to maintain symmetry as much as possible.

08: DIRECT EYE CONTACT

Direct eye contact lets the interviewer know you're confident and have no problem talking face-to-face. Maybe you've heard "When he talks to you, it's like you're the only person in the room." That's because the person they're talking to uses direct eye contact the correct way.

Do it the wrong way and you might make the person you're talking to feel uncomfortable. What's the wrong way? *Not* breaking eye contact, holding your gaze too long, and not blinking very often. Constant direct eye contact with a low blink rate is a pre-violence cue that makes the other person's limbic system say, "Hang on a second . . . Something's not right here."

Proper direct eye contact, as seen in the example picture, is executed with what I call "Soft Eye Contact." That is maintaining eye contact, pulling your eyebrows upward every now and then to show the "I'm listening" cue, and breaking eye contact and blinking when it's appropriate. This may not sound important, but when executed the right way, direct eye contact makes all the difference in the world.

09: OPEN-HANDED GESTURING AND BODY SYMMETRY

Whether you're talking to one person or 1,500 people, open-handed gesturing is a powerful tool. In the example picture, we see this gesturing used to make the interviewer's brain see something it absolutely loves to see. What is it? Symmetry.

We see it in advertisements, art, nature, and even in some of the most beautiful and handsome faces in the world. Of the seven universal facial expressions, all but one is symmetrical—that one outlier being Contempt.

As the interviewee is answering questions, they use their illustrators together, in sync, creating a symmetrical picture that helps keep the interviewer's attention. Although this can look odd if you're not careful, it's important to create an invisible frame or box for yourself. Bill Clinton used what's known as "The Clinton Box." Most of his open-handed gestures were used in an invisible box he created between his chest and navel. Mark

Bowden suggests using something similar that he coined "The Truth Plane," which is the horizontal plane right at navel height.

10: ELBOWS ANCHORED TO TABLE

Anchored elbows tell you two things:

1. The person anchoring is confident with the subject being discussed.

2. They are in control of what's being related to the other person. In other words, they are creating a picture with details of the subject they are explaining or telling the other person.

When a person's elbows are anchored, it doesn't mean that they never move or that the person anchors them as soon as they sit down. This is one of those things that must be finessed. You'll notice that, as they use their open-handed gestures to create symmetry (as we discussed earlier), they will anchor one elbow, talk for a bit, and then anchor the other elbow to create a base for their hands to illustrate from. The picture here shows a great example of that.

When the elbows are anchored, it's also the perfect opportunity to steeple the fingers, and you'll see that quite often. Not so much as to look arrogant, but they will steeple enough to add to the other cues that are showing a degree of solid confidence.

HOW TO KNOW WHEN A JOB INTERVIEW IS NOT GOING WELL

Have you ever come out of a job interview and thought, "Yes! That couldn't have gone any better," only to find out two weeks later that somebody else got the gig? What about the opposite? You just knew things didn't go well, so you kept looking at other places. Both are quite common, but the first one hurts. If you're watching a job interview, there are several things that will let you know things aren't going very well.

Most likely, the first cue you'll spot is slouching posture. You can't miss it. Even at a distance, it stands out like a house on fire. Noticing the slouched posture is usually followed by the lowered head. This cue can indicate everything from sadness to defeat. A person's head is probably lowered due to their limbic system protecting their throat. When we feel threatened, we will lower our head to get our chin in front of the neck so that our aggressor can't get to it.

Since you're already looking at the head, check out the eyebrows. When they're pulled toward the middle and up just a bit, this denotes physical or emotional pain. In this case, you're seeing emotional pain.

Let's move down the face to the mouth. Here's where you'll see one of three things happening with the mouth. The lips will have completely disappeared, pursed, or they will be pursed to one side. If the lips are compressed, that is the Stress Mouth we discussed in chapter 3 and you're most likely seeing a load of stress. The person may also be trying to keep their thoughts to themself and not speak.

Maybe the lips are pursed. This is quite common when someone doesn't agree with what is happening, what was just said, or what's being presented to them. In this case, it's probably the realization that the interviewer doesn't think that the candidate's the one for the job. What if the lips are pursed to the side? This suggests that they see a different outcome to what has just happened or to what is happening. You'll see this happen at the golf course when it's obvious a putt isn't going exactly where it should be going. The golfer's lips will purse to one side as the ball just grazes the hole.

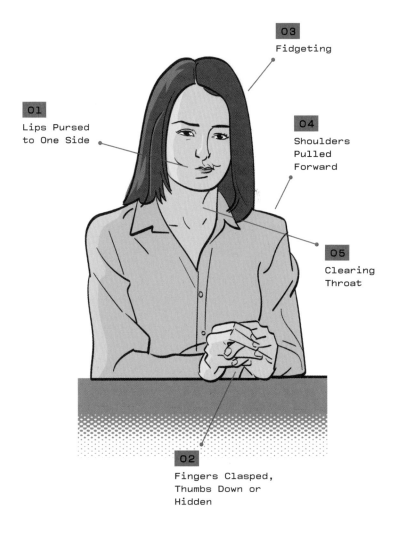

03
Fidgeting

01
Lips Pursed
to One Side

04
Shoulders
Pulled
Forward

05
Clearing
Throat

02
Fingers Clasped,
Thumbs Down or
Hidden

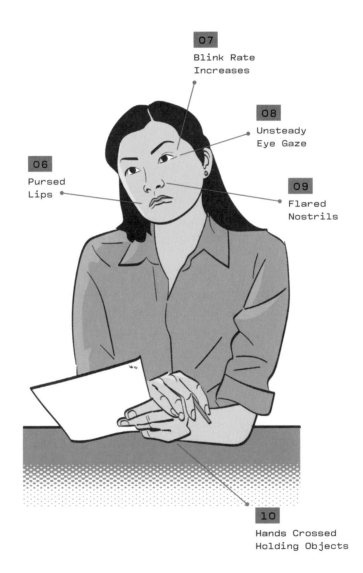

07

Blink Rate
Increases

08

Unsteady
Eye Gaze

06

Pursed
Lips

09

Flared
Nostrils

10

Hands Crossed
Holding Objects

01: LIPS PURSED TO ONE SIDE

When we observe pursed lips, we can be fairly confident in assuming that person is in disagreement or has an issue with the subject matter at hand. The lips pursed to one side suggests disagreement as well. However, it also suggests that the person sees a different outcome than what has just happened or is happening in that moment.

For example, watch someone who is new to bowling. When they let the ball go and it's headed for the gutter, you'll likely see their lips purse to one side, enough so that it changes the entire look of their face. In their mind, they see the ball staying in the lane. The same goes for the pro bowler after they miss an important strike. The bowler may remain calm, but may purse their lips to the side for several seconds, having expected a different outcome. In the example picture, the interviewee feels the interview isn't going as well as they had hoped it would go before it began. Hence, lips pursed to one side.

02: FINGERS CLASPED, THUMBS DOWN OR HIDDEN

Hands close together with the fingers tightly clasped suggests the person has very little confidence about the situation they're dealing with. When you add the thumbs drawn down or hidden and the wrists pulled close together, as in the example picture, you've got a cocktail of low confidence, shame, and possibly fear. Not fear suggesting physical harm, but fear that the chances of saving this situation are zero.

Tightly clasped fingers may be the last indicator you notice in the chain of cues leading you to them. Here's why. When you first observe this situation—remember, this happens very quickly—you will look at the head and face. You will register those cues as you move to the neck, then to the shoulders. You will add those cues to the facial cues as you sweep down the arms. While measuring and taking in those cues, you will see the hands. You will add those cues to the ones you've gathered and start making your final decisions, depending on whether or not you can see the legs and feet.

03: FIDGETING

One thing I train people to look for is which person moves the least in the meeting or at the table. This goes for board meetings and lunch meetings, as well as negotiations. This behavior usually signifies that that person is the alpha or is in a leadership position in that group. That person's movements will be intentional and smooth. This gives them the air of being focused, in control of themselves, and gives the feeling that they're the one you need to pay attention to and listen to.

When you see someone continuously and awkwardly adjusting in their chair, it suggests they are uncomfortable or are having a hard time accepting what is being talked about or presented. When a job interview is not going well, the interviewee is thinking many things. They're most likely running different scenarios about what to do and say next to help fix the situation. They may be thinking about alternatives to the job the interviewer is talking to them about. Whatever the reason, it lets the observer know there's an issue here.

04: SHOULDERS PULLED FORWARD

If I asked you to look like you've been let down or to look depressed, the first thing you would do is put the classic kid's frown on your face, hang your head down, and slump your shoulders forward. Ta-dah! You look like a six-year-old who can't have any cookies before dinner.

When a job interview is going south, you may see this same thing but to a much lesser degree. This shoulder cue indicates they've lost or are losing their confidence. As their shoulders slump forward, their torso tends to bend forward and down. You may also notice something quite odd: They may look as though they're slowly getting shorter and shorter. That's common in a situation like this. As the interviewee's confidence grows smaller, they may slowly begin lowering themselves in their chair.

You'll also notice less movement from the interviewee and their answers will grow quieter as the interview continues. With their shoulders continuing to pull forward and drop, their lack of confidence will become more and more obvious.

05: CLEARING THROAT

Clearing an itchy throat because there's something in it is normal behavior, and it sounds normal. It will be a little loud and the person may put their hand up to cover their mouth. They might even say, "Excuse me" or, "Sorry about that." It may happen again soon after if the clearing didn't work, and if it continues, they will most likely take a drink or ask for some water. We've all seen and been in this situation.

Then you have the throat clearing that indicates stress and/or nervousness. It's similar to what you may see and hear when someone is being deceptive and feels things aren't going well with their story. Their throat gets dry and itchy as they begin breathing deeper and a little heavier, and the clearing becomes more of a short, muffled bark kind of sound. It's not as loud as normal throat clearing and it happens every 15 to 20 seconds or every minute or so. In this situation, it suggests that the interviewee is nervous and knows things aren't going well.

06: PURSED LIPS

In this example, we see pursed lips. As we discussed earlier, this suggests there is disagreement with what is being said or presented. We're all familiar with the pursed lips a child exhibits when angry or not getting their way, and there's nothing subtle about it. However, as we grow older and begin reining in our facial expressions so as not to let others know exactly what's on our mind or what we're feeling, pursed lips become something you almost have to specifically look for.

In civil conversations involving uncomfortable subjects, full-blown pursed lips almost never pop out at us, not enough to notice anyway. On the other hand, as in the example above, there are occasions when they are slightly pursed for a short period. Then there are the occasions when they are pursed for quite a while, indicating that person is entrenched in their disagreement or unwillingness to accept the situation. The example here suggests the interviewer is disappointed and has already made the decision that this is not the person for her company to hire.

07: BLINK RATE INCREASES

In the situation pictured on page 105, when the interviewer's blink rate increases, it most likely suggests that they've decided this interviewee isn't everything they hoped for and they won't be hiring them. As the interviewer's inner dialogue focuses on who the next interviewee in line may be, their brain becomes a bit uncomfortable knowing they must sit there for another few minutes listening to someone talking and wasting their time. Keep in mind, this may not be exactly how they feel, and the interviewer is not preparing to be rude, but they're finished talking with this person and are looking for a properly timed conversational "out" to bring things to a close quickly so they can move on.

Another possible reason for a sudden increase in her blink rate may be that the interviewee has hit on a subject that's uncomfortable for the interviewer and is seeing that person attempt to control their reaction as they become irritated. Or it could possibly mean they've hit on something very interesting to the interviewer and they are developing a question or questions to ask next.

08: UNSTEADY EYE GAZE

The proper use of eye gazing is one of the most powerful skills anyone can hone. You can make someone angry, doubt themselves, doubt you, engage with you, keep looking at you, and even tell you things they hadn't planned on telling you, all just by looking at them a certain way.

When you're being interviewed, the interviewer should be interested not only in your answers, but in *how* you answer. They're looking for your level of confidence in what they know is a bit of a stressful situation. If they're interested, you will notice their blink rate slow down. They will stay focused on you. Their brain will want to take in as much information as possible about you as you answer.

It's human nature to keep our eyes on whatever it is we're interested in. If you notice an unsteady gaze or the interviewer looking behind you, out the door or window, and/or at their computer screen or watch every few minutes, something's up.

09: FLARED NOSTRILS

Most people are under the impression that flared nostrils only indicate anger and/or aggression. You will definitely see them flare when the situation grows tense or leans toward possible violence, but there's a reason for that. For example, when we watch an argument, we'll see flared nostrils. When we watch the Boston Marathon, we'll see flared nostrils. When we watch a boxing match, we'll see flared nostrils. What does this tell us? It lets us know that the brain is sending extra oxygen to the muscles to prepare them for the task at hand.

Quite often, when we see compressed lips or Stress Mouth, we'll see flared nostrils as well. That indicates that person is holding back information. They may want to say something but they know they can't or shouldn't, or they're waiting for the right moment to speak. Taking into consideration all of the other cues we're seeing in the example, that's most likely what we're seeing. The interviewer has decided that this person doesn't fit the job description and she's waiting for the right time to let her know.

10: HANDS CROSSED HOLDING OBJECTS

This is one of those cues that let you know the interviewer needs more than they are getting from the interviewee. It's not a good sign because they are creating a barrier not only with their hands and arms, but also with the paper or object they're holding.

Another important cue we see is the position of the right hand over the left wrist. When a person feels positive toward or attracted to the person they're speaking with, they will often display their wrists or leave them uncovered. In this situation, we're not seeing them displayed, as both of them are hidden.

Also, the interviewer's arm is extended, placing the paper further away from them, almost like it's a bag of dog poop that they don't want anywhere near them. Is this the interviewee's résumé? If so, this is probably the worst nonverbal cue the interviewer can exhibit. It suggests they want it as far away from themselves as possible. This, combined with all of the other negative cues we've seen up this point, suggests this poor interviewee isn't getting hired today.

HOW TO KEEP THE
INTERVIEW POSITIVE

If an interview goes bad, you might not realize it until it's almost over. Even though you may see many of cues we've gone over that let you know the waters are getting rough, they may not register in your brain. You must start searching for them at the beginning of the meeting.

If you see pursed lips, you probably said something the interviewer doesn't agree with or sees differently. For example, you may have said, " . . . and I always do it that way." To fix it, you might add, "But now, my approach is a bit different . . . " If the interviewer is using both hands as barriers, use a trick my BFF, homicide detective Jason Rosalia, taught me. Hand the inter- viewer something, anything, to make them use their hands. It breaks the barrier and you can continue from there.

If you notice flared nostrils, slowly take in a semi-deep breath and let it out even slower as they talk. Begin your answer to the question as you turn on that slow and tiny smile. Their mirror neurons will fire and their nostril flaring will exit as a small smile enters. (If you remember nothing else about correcting a bad situation, remember the slow, tiny smile.)

If you notice an increased blink rate, they're thinking hard and fast. It's time to break that train of thought and ask a ques- tion. Choose wisely which question you ask, but ask *something*. When things are headed south in an interview, don't panic. You can turn it around 90 percent of the time.

SIX:

MASTERING THE LANDSCAPE OF YOUR WORKPLACE

ANY OFFICE ENVIRONMENT contains a variety of many different personalities and personality types. For the body language enthusiast, amateur or pro, it's the gift that keeps on giving. The more people there are that work there, the more wonderful the gift becomes. You've got introverts who must interact with extroverts. You've got the bossy personality type that talks too loudly to the grumpy personality type. These situations always prove to be gold mines for those interested in nonverbal communication.

One of my favorite situations is the know-it-all telling the closet genius what they'd do if they were president of the company. The genius stands there and listens while showing their disdain with every nonverbal and facial cue possible and it goes right over the know-it-all's head. Then, there's the all-around great employee. They're a good person but miss the cues that tell them that their partner on the new project has no idea what is happening or what the project is about, then the good employee blows their top when the partner adds nothing helpful to the project. If they had known what the lips pursed to the side and the tilted head indicated, they wouldn't have this problem. Understanding just the basics of nonverbal communication can make everyone's office experience so much more pleasant.

GETTING A SENSE FOR WORKPLACE PERSONALITIES

There are many different personality types in the workplace. They vary from company to company, but there's one thing you can count on. You're always going to have four or five of the "classic" personalities most everyone is aware of. These include the Bore, the Know-It-All, the Big Personality, the Content Employee, the Cranky Employee, the Power-Hungry Employee, the Shy Person, the Agitator, the Friend, the Shallow Friend, and the Gossip, among others.

Some of these are easy to spot, while others may take a while to uncover. You'll most likely discover the Shallow Friend personality first. They are a combination of a Walmart greeter and the mailman. They love meeting you, and the greeting you get every day is cordial and very friendly, but it's the same and never goes any further than that. The Know-It-All is my favorite. No matter what you talk about, bring up, or do, they're going to know all about it and they're going to tell you how to do it better. They're not bad people. They just want to help *waaaay* too much. You'll see lots of confidence cues from this person.

Be nice to the Gossip. They will spread any rumor they hear and do their best to make sure everyone is aware of it. The Power-Hungry personality will use this person to their advantage as the Gossip strategically feeds them information they want others to know or "learn" about themselves or someone else. The Agitator will use the Gossip in a similar fashion, only to stir things up and cause discord among others.

The Content personality will be the one you enjoy the most. They will always be pleasant and have great things to say about anyone and everyone. They may be a little kinesthetic or touchy-feely. They'll be the one to pat your hand or congratulate you with a hug. They are always smiling and are the equivalent of having a living flower in the office. The Cranky personality is their opposite. You'll notice what I call "Half-Bad Posture." That means their posture isn't the worst, but it's on its way. They will despise their nemesis, the Content personality. But that's okay—they despise most everything and everyone, so at least they are consistent. In spite of this, their work will be top-notch and the CEO will tolerate them because of that.

The Bore will love to talk and tend to focus on things that interest only themselves. If you don't spot this person when you first arrive, you're going to be in for a couple of horrifically boring lunches. They will be open and use big hand gestures, yet their voice will be at a low volume and there will be little or no excitement in their delivery.

Keep in mind, there's nothing wrong with any of these personality types. You just need to know that others experience them as well and they are in no way unique to your office. Take a bit of time to reflect on whether or not you fall into one of these categories . . . because other people are certainly considering it.

THE AGITATOR

In every office or business, there's always that one troublemaker known as "The Agitator." They may not actually be making trouble. Most of the time, you could more accurately call them the "Problem Creator." They're the one that takes most of the bagels on Friday mornings and doesn't refill the coffee maker. Whether they're young or old, male or female: There's always an Agitator.

The Agitator is an observant person. You'll notice them hanging around in the back before the meeting starts and they're usually the last one to sit down. If there's food, they'll be eating throughout the meeting. Not unlike a shoplifter trying to make themselves smaller by keeping their hands and arms close and almost hunching over as they walk, when the Agitator has troublemaking on their mind, that'll be the behavior you'll most likely see from them. You may also notice that their head remains still as their eyes scan the room. They're not going to steal anything. They're just laying low in case a troublemaking opportunity presents itself.

THE INSECURE EMPLOYEE

The Insecure Employee will either be one of the first of these personalities you discover at the office or one of the last. When there is a situation that causes people to react immediately (such as a request for a volunteer), if there's a fire drill, or if there's an announcement that there's birthday cake for everybody in the breakroom, I always pay attention to the person who reacts or moves last. Those moments can tell you so much about a person and their mindset.

The Insecure person doesn't want attention. You won't see them engage in direct eye contact for more time than is absolutely necessary, and they will almost never touch another person. By that, I mean they won't initiate a high-five, they will make sure they never brush up against someone getting into or out of the elevator, and they probably won't introduce themselves to you and offer a handshake. Their clothing style will be almost drab. However, you may see a splash of brighter clothing once in a blue moon, when they are feeling a bit more secure.

THE DISGRUNTLED EMPLOYEE

One of the first things you'll notice about the Unhappy or Disgruntled Employee is their lack of involvement in most everything at work. Their facial expression will often be sullen, with plenty of compressed and pursed lips. These cues indicate the employee is holding back regarding what they're thinking about saying or doing. Continuously showing up late for work and for meetings is another set of red flags to look for. The main theme of conversation will typically focus on how bad the boss or the company is or how bad the other employees are.

Negativity will flow both verbally and nonverbally. You may spot them rolling their eyes when the boss or person in charge speaks, not just to them but to others as well. This employee will take way too many breaks each day and they will talk too much about looking for another job or seeking out a better situation. They'll talk about their gloomy financial situation. One thing to be very cautious of is dismissing any kind of talk you may hear from this person about being violent or hinting about doing something "everyone will hear about." These comments should be taken seriously, and you should go to HR with your concerns immediately.

THE CONTENT EMPLOYEE

The Content Employee will be pleasant and speak with a pleasant tone, not just in person but on the phone as well. They will dress in brighter colors and have a well put-together look. More often than not, their illustrators will be large. They will be open to conversation, the themes will be pleasant and positive, and their stories will usually focus on their family.

The Content Employee will partake early in the bagel and donut offerings and will often bring cards or treats for special occasions. If their space is a cubicle, more often than not they will smile before they turn to look outside of the cubicle. Their eyebrows will be up and remain up as they scan the work area or meeting room. They want to connect and talk when it's appropriate. At lunchtime, they will be part of a group, no matter whether they stay and eat or go out for lunch. Their desk and work area will be clean, straight, and have photos and maybe a plant or two. Their area will also have decorations for holidays. Expressions of anger or sadness are few and far between.

THE POWER-HUNGRY EMPLOYEE

You'll find this office-type to be a rule follower and they're going to want you to follow those rules as well. They've read the books and they're under the impression that they have a pretty good handle on "leadership." That's what makes them tend to be a bit bossy. They will dress in a similar fashion to the boss. If the boss wears strict business attire, you can expect the same from the Power-Hungry employee.

They have no problem with direct eye contact, and you'll hear them refer to the boss by name once or twice a day. They will see themselves as next in line for that big promotion. They may address everyone in the office as "Mr. ____" and "Miss/Mrs. ____" to sound professional. You will notice approving smiles and nods when they say things like "Working hard today?" or "How's the Johnson report coming along?" They may even tell you to "Keep up the good work" after your presentation at the meeting. The easiest way to get along with the Power-Hungry Employee is to appease their ego.

HOW TO PROJECT CONFIDENCE IN THE WORKPLACE

There are many types and styles of personalities in the workplace. Fitting in and getting along with all of them isn't impossible, but sometimes this can make things a bit tough, especially if your confidence is running on the low side. However, there are body language and nonverbal cues you can use to solidify your spot as a confident person.

1. **EYE CONTACT.** This is one of the most potent cues. Don't be afraid to make eye contact and keep it when talking to someone. You're going to have to break eye contact every so often, so you don't look like a psychopath—that's fine. Just be sure to connect visually.

2. **SPEAKING VOICE.** Be sure you speak loud enough to be heard clearly. It may seem odd and too loud at first, but the last thing you want is people asking you to speak up.

3. **SMILE.** Even if it's a small smile, it indicates you're in control and that everything is okay.

4. **OWN YOUR SPACE.** One thing I train teachers to look for is the child who doesn't look around much. They don't "own" the space around them. This denotes shyness and insecurity. Don't be afraid to look around the room and connect with a smile or head nod.

5. **TALK TO PEOPLE.** Speak to anyone within a 6-foot radius. Try saying "Hello", "How are you today?", or "How are you doing?" when you speak first and when you're in charge of the conversation. People notice this more often than you think.

There are plenty more cues you can use, but these five will get you started toward feeling confident in your workplace.

HOW TO INTERPRET A CLIENT PITCH

From 2011 until 2017, I was the Entrepreneur in Residence at the Nashville Entrepreneur Center. During that time, I trained hundreds of entrepreneurs to create investor pitches. I still help entrepreneurs create pitches. To this day, *every* person I've trained to create an Investable Pitch has been funded, to the tune of $480 million.

The key to the Investable Pitch is the body language the entrepreneur uses throughout the pitch, and believe me, it's specific and tactical. By that, I mean that they engage their body language tools immediately; even before entering the office of the possible investor(s).

By that same token, I'm hired by investors and venture capitalists to watch entrepreneurs pitch and let them know what I think about the behavior I'm observing. Is the entrepreneur being honest? Trustworthy? Will they try to do what they say they will? Do they really believe in the idea, product, or service? When the entrepreneur reaches the financial section of the pitch, what does their body language say? Are they comfortable? Are they unsure? Do they step back a quarter of a step? Does the volume of their voice change at all? Who do they look at when explaining why these financials are valid? Do their eyes kick over to the CFO and back? Do they look at the COO and stay for a moment and then return to the investors? These are valid questions, and each has its own meaning.

When the new startup's CEO first reaches the financial section of the pitch and steps or leans back, this suggests they are unsure. It does *not* mean they are being dishonest. It simply suggests they are unsure about the financials. That's why you want to pay attention to see if they look at anyone specific at that point. If they quickly look over at the CFO, you're probably dealing with a situation where they got the information from the CFO but haven't actually done the math themselves. So, it would make sense, if the scenario is as it seems, that they may be unsure about what they're telling the investors about the financials.

Some would say that this situation would be bad for the startup, but that is not necessarily true. It may be showing you their concern that they may not be giving you the correct information. You'll want to ask questions like "Did you go deep into the financials yourself?" (Keep in mind, they should have because they're the CEO and that's part of their job, especially when pitching.) If they say, "I haven't yet but our CFO, Mike, can answer any questions you may have in detail." This indicates they're being honest. That's good.

If the CFO steps up and you begin asking them questions and they take a quick look at the COO every few minutes, you may have a situation involving deception on their part. Why are they looking at the COO? When pitching, there are many nonverbals that will create trust. There are even more that will destroy that trust. Let's take a closer look at both.

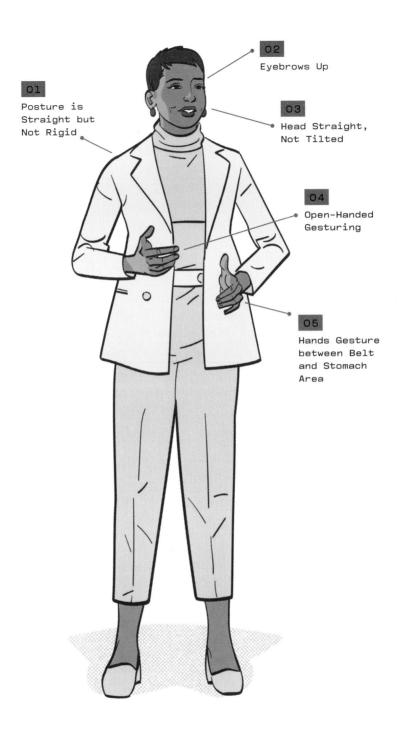

01
Posture is
Straight but
Not Rigid

02
Eyebrows Up

03
Head Straight,
Not Tilted

04
Open-Handed
Gesturing

05
Hands Gesture
between Belt
and Stomach
Area

01: POSTURE IS STRAIGHT BUT NOT RIGID

Good posture is a must when pitching. However, good posture doesn't mean your back is as straight and rigid as a broom handle. "Good" means "proper," and there's no place you want your posture to be more proper than when you're trying to convince investors to invest or when trying to convince those at work to adopt your ideas or plan.

When you watch an entrepreneur or colleague pitch, you want them to look relaxed and to feel confident. If they look nervous, bells and whistles go off in your head and you stop listening. When their posture is rigid, the rest of their body movements look insincere and forced.

The key to having straight but not rigid posture during a pitch is to take the biggest breath you can and hold it. That's rigid posture. Let the air out slowly then take a quick in-and-out breath. That's straight but *not* rigid posture. That trick works like a charm every time.

02: EYEBROWS UP

One of the keys to a successful investor pitch is knowing how to use your eyebrows correctly. The "Eyebrows Up" cue commands attention in a subtle way. This is similar to the "Eyebrow Flash." That's what you do when you're in the grocery store and see someone three aisles away that you know from work. Your eyebrows flash up, then back down as your head goes back and forward in a quick nod. You're saying, "Hi there! We know each other!" without saying a word.

During the pitch, the entrepreneur must randomly choose one of the investors every two minutes or so and Eyebrow Flash them, without the head nod of course. This makes the investor's brain say, "Hey, they know me . . . I guess I know them." It's not a conscious thought, but it puts the suggestion in there and grabs their attention.

When you see this in a pitch, it indicates the entrepreneur is trying to connect with you as they pitch you their idea.

03: HEAD STRAIGHT, NOT TILTED

When pitching an idea, the presenter is the one in charge and is telling those listening the way things are. Tilting the head to one side is the "I'm listening" cue. There's a time for the head tilt during the pitch process. However, during the actual pitch is not that place.

When pitching, the presenter's head and body must be as symmetrical as possible. This shows balance and gives the presenter the air of control and of being in charge. The head tilted back can be a poison dart to a pitch, as this gives the presenter that infamous look of arrogance.

When the head is tilted forward, that is usually a display of aggression or subservience. You want neither of these. The aggressive attitude is usually met in kind from the investors or from others in the meeting if it is an idea for your company. Subservience is the last thing the presenter wants noticed. People want to listen to and invest in the person in charge, not the person who's there to please everyone.

04: OPEN-HANDED GESTURING

We've covered hand gestures quite a bit, and now you understand there's more to it than just gesturing with your hands open. When you combine different styles of open-handed gesturing with other body language cues, you begin to create a powerful combination of indicators that put you in charge for the duration of the pitch or presentation.

In a pitch, it's important to make sure the fingers of the presenter have some space between them. You'll remember we talked about this when we covered how to know when a date is going well (see page 74). Space between the fingers lets you know the presenter is relaxed, not worried, and that they're prepared. When there is space between the fingers, there will be space between the tips of the fingers and the palms as well.

Keep in mind, people don't think the person who fails to use open-handed gestures when pitching or presenting is a deviant or a con, but using open-handed gestures with plenty of space between the fingers suggests openness and gives off an air of honesty.

05: HANDS GESTURE BETWEEN BELT AND STOMACH AREA

We talk about hand gestures so much because it's important to have an understanding of the many different situations in which you can use them. When you watch the world's most persuasive speakers in action, you'll see them gesture 80 to 90 percent of the time in the area between the belt and the stomach. No matter what country or culture they're from, they will gesture from this "plane" or "box."

Why do we feel we can trust the person using this cue? There are several reasons. They are exposing their stomach and chest area. This shows they have no weapons, no fear of harm, and nothing to hide. These movements also follow the symmetrical "pattern" you want to convey to those watching.

Consider this: The presenters of TED Talks with the greatest amount of views all use open-handed gestures almost the entire time they are speaking. Keep in mind, a pitch is the "Big Game" for entrepreneurs and presenters, so using persuasive body language cues—especially open-handed gestures—is their key to a successful presentation.

HOW TO DECIPHER WHAT'S REALLY BEING SAID IN YOUR ANNUAL REVIEW

Whether you've been on the job for one year or ten years, you're going to have an annual review. You want to make sure the reasons you are there are obvious to the reviewer. There will be plenty of questions and you will need to decode their nonverbals to determine what they're really saying and feeling so you can answer appropriately.

During the process, there will be questions about mistakes that you've made, usually one in particular. When they ask the question about the mistake, are they coming in hot by looking you directly in the eye with no change in the movement of their arms, hands, or facial expression? If that's the case, this is a big deal. They've braced themselves and are listening and watching closely for your reaction.

They're going to have a checklist with a combination of questions they ask everyone and then questions they're only asking you. The questions they're asking everyone will be the ones they won't spend much time on. Those are going to be the yes or no questions they'll just check off as you go. Of course, some will require more detailed answers, but stick with the less-is-more approach to these questions. With some of these, they may not even look up. They may literally just check them off and move on to the next one. It's the speed with which they ask the question that's important in these cases.

If they ask quickly without looking up, it's probably not that important. But if they stare at the question and pause before they look up to ask it, this one is important. They have quickly run the scenario they're going to ask about in their head and they are going to want a good answer. This is where you use the open-handed gestures we've talked so much about when providing your answer. You want to remain as still as possible while answering, but not so still that you look weird or like a statue. You want to look centered, symmetrical, and in control.

When you finish answering, they're going to say something like "Okay" while they nod their head and then move on to the next question, or their eyebrows will go up and their bottom lip will push their upper lip up as they nod. This is good. The scenario they ran through their head before asking the question has played out, they see what happened, and they accept it. This is when you turn on a small smile. Doing so will subconsciously solidify the feeling for them that the subject has come to a close.

You'll be able to get a pretty good idea of how things really went by the way they act during your "wrap-up" conversation. If their comments and asides are short without much eye contact, something is bothering them. If you get good, clean, eye contact and you see cues of relaxation, lots of space between the fingers, a real smile, and a lower tone of voice, you can look forward to next year's review.

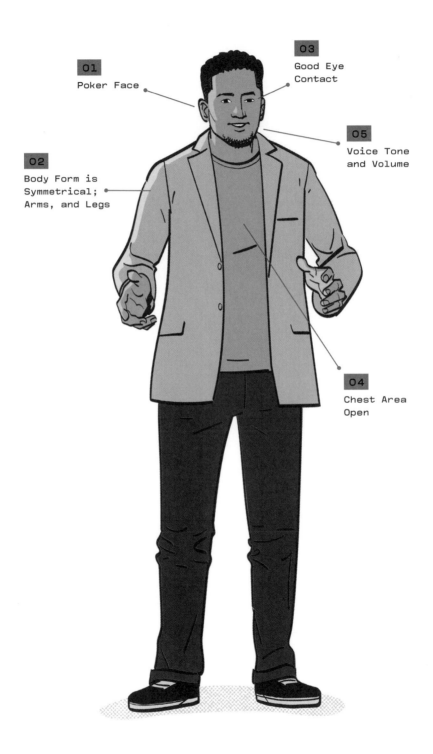

01
Poker Face

03
Good Eye
Contact

05
Voice Tone
and Volume

02
Body Form is
Symmetrical;
Arms, and Legs

04
Chest Area
Open

01: POKER FACE

You'll see the "poker face" in movies when the hero knows exactly what to do when the problem arrives. An expressionless look while presenting relays confidence and gives those watching the feeling that they are observing someone who knows what they're talking about and who can turn their ideas into reality.

However, there is a caveat here. If the presenter shows no emotion at all, those watching will feel that around the 10-minute mark. A constant show of no emotion can signal fear. That means that engaging the slow and tiny smile for 15 to 20 seconds, every 5 to 7 minutes, is imperative. This reminds those watching that the presenter is human, has emotions, and is approachable.

If the presenter stops talking and just stands there and smiles for the 15 to 20 seconds, it won't end well. But if they pause for a second and begin talking as the tiny smile slowly grows, the mirror neurons in the brains of those watching will fire and they will begin to smile and feel that positive emotion as well.

02: BODY FORM IS SYMMETRICAL

The human brain demands to see symmetry in a leader. When a presenter stands straight, feet shoulder-width apart, the arms illustrating evenly, and with the head straight, they are spot-on for being seen as a confident leader.

When the feet are shoulder-width apart, that's the Legs Akimbo stance we discussed earlier (see page 50). Leaders and those in charge stand that way. Police officers, members of the military, and professional fighters and boxers all stand that way. It indicates you have great confidence when you take that stance. However, you must do it correctly. If you go too wide, you'll look goofy. If you don't go wide enough, you'll just look like everyone else.

Keep in mind, you don't want to stand with Legs Akimbo all the time. That will give others the feeling you are overbearing. It could also turn that feeling of confidence you want to relay into an air of arrogance that is difficult to correct.

03: GOOD EYE CONTACT

One of the first things you'll notice when speaking to someone with little or no self-confidence is that they avoid lengthy eye contact. Eye contact is an iffy subject anyway. If you don't keep eye contact long enough, they'll think you can't do the job or that your interest is low. If you look them in the eye too long, they may think you're aggressive or that maybe you are attracted to them. Eye contact is really about balance.

How do you know how long is too long or not long enough? It's something you will feel. You will know it's right when it feels right. Psychopaths don't have the ability to empathize. In other words, they can't relate to how you feel about anything at all. That's why you hear people talk about psychopaths retro-spectively saying, "He looked at me from across the room and just wouldn't stop." Or, "He had a stare that was creepy every time we talked." A psycho-path doesn't know that cut-off point once the eye contact is too long. You're not a psychopath—that's why you feel it.

04: CHEST AREA OPEN

You and your best friend went out for dinner. Afterwards, you both go back to your place because your friend left her keys on your kitchen table. You unlock and open the front door. The room is dark and very quiet, almost scary. You slowly walk in . . . and before you reach the light switch, you hear a crowd yell "Surprise! Happy Birthday!" as all the lights pop on. What do your hands do at that moment? They fly up to your chest to protect your heart and lungs. You can't help it. Everyone does it. That's your limbic system switching into Freeze, Fight, or Flight mode.

When presenting, you don't stand there with your hands up protecting your face like someone is going to throw something at you. That would not only make you look odd, but those watching your presentation would never take you seriously. Keeping your hands and arms away from your chest area, leaving it open, on a subconscious level tells others you're not afraid and that you're confident not just with the situation, but with them as well.

05: VOICE TONE AND VOLUME

Once these other body language cues of confidence we covered are in place, the cue that takes it in for a touchdown is your voice tone and volume. Most people think, "You just speak clearly and loudly enough for people to hear." That's like describing how to win the gold medal in the Olympic speed skating event by saying, "Just skate faster and more skillfully than all of the other best skaters in the world." If you speak too clearly, you're going to sound like something's wrong with you. If you speak too loudly, it's going to sound like you're yelling.

Speaking to a group with confidence is an art. Whether or not you *are* confident doesn't enter into it. You just have to *sound* confident. As for volume, if you think you're loud enough, you probably aren't. Speak to the back row. Don't yell; speak loudly and push air using your stomach instead of your throat. There's nothing that shows confidence more than a solid voice tone that everyone can hear and understand. It just takes practice.

HOW TO ANALYZE THE COMPANY MEETING

As a human behavior enthusiast, this meeting will become your absolute favorite. Depending on the size of the company, the number of people in the meeting will vary. Let's use a smaller number, but big enough to fill a large boardroom with a big table. This meeting will have a plethora of cliques, leaders, wannabe leaders, Content employees, Power-Hungry employees . . . You name it and that personality type, with all of its specific body language cues, will be there.

First, let's take a look at the CEO. When they move, the movements will be smooth and intentional. By that, I mean you won't see those small, quick, jerky movements you'll see younger employees or new hires make throughout the meeting. You'll find that the CEO will be the one who moves the least. They won't remain motionless like a statue, but their movements will have purpose. You've seen this while observing from your old point of view, but you probably didn't realize it.

Let's move to the person next to the CEO's chair. The person to their right is going to be the person who is, or wants to be, the "right-hand person." Usually, it's the COO. This person will want to show everyone that, if the CEO is unavailable, they'll be there, and everything will be just fine. Similar to the CEO, you won't see much movement or many cues from their area. They'll remain calm, with not much to say outside of regular meeting subjects. You won't see this person raise their hand to be recognized by the CEO—they'll do that with a look or raise of their eyebrows and by throwing their index finger up (a regulator). When the CEO gives the go-ahead, they'll speak.

When the long-term employees engage in their questions or statements, they will be at a proper volume and they will get directly to the point. Their hands will be on the table, sometimes along with their entire forearm. You'll see them take up a bit more table real estate than the new hires. However, it will be their hands and arms that inhabit that space because the area around them is malleable. In other words, they may need to move them to make room for the person next to them to use their hands and arms as they speak. In the case of the CEO and COO, their real estate will be taken up by their computer, a notebook, and/or folders. This space is understood to be impenetrable by everyone at the table.

The new hires will most likely stay quiet and will not add much, if anything, to the meeting, unless they are asked to do so. They will sit up straight with their feet on the floor and you'll most likely see several preening adjustments of clothing and attire throughout the meeting as they try to maintain their "professionalism" as best as they can. This begins wearing off about eight to ten months into the job.

01
Eyes Squinting

03
Wrinkles on
Forehead

02
Gesturing with
Open Hands

04
Small Smile
(The Slow and
Tiny Smile)

05
Fingers
Lightly Rubbing
Together

01: EYES SQUINTING

When someone squints, it can mean several different things. It may indicate what's known as Eye Blocking, which we do when we view something we find distasteful or vulgar. Or, the squinter may be experiencing pain or receiving bad news. However, what we see in this situation is the good kind of squinting. It lets us know that they're trying to understand what's being said and are focusing on every word. Similar to the way we squint when trying to read a road sign at a distance, they are squinting so they can make sure that they understand every bit of information given by the person speaking.

There are several other things that must be happening at the same time to let us know that this is a good squint. The person's head should be tilted to the side in a listening position, and this should be accompanied by a slow head nod every 10 to 15 seconds. If the squint is so engaged you can hardly see the eyes, that's not good. That's the squint that accompanies profound doubt.

02: GESTURING WITH OPEN HANDS

Once again, open-handed gestures come into play. This style is a bit different though. When someone emphasizes words or phrases with their hands, they are using illustrators. There is another gesture style that may look similar, but the meanings are very different. In the example, we see what is known as a regulator. Regulators are used to control situations, such as to stop someone from talking, let someone know they are next, or to call a timeout in football by making the "T" symbol with one's hands.

We also use them to slow down or speed up conversations. In this example, the reviewer is using a regulator to pause the conversation for a moment to either go back and have something repeated or to add something of importance to the information being given. Sometimes an adaptor will be held in place while the person gives an opinion or thought. When held in place, the regulator is most likely being used in an aggressive manner, but not in this case. In this case, it pops up and retreats quickly.

03: WRINKLES ON FOREHEAD

The great thing about the forehead is that it gives us a pretty good idea of what emotion a person is experiencing, even from a distance. As long as we can see the forehead, we'll know if that person is angry, happy, sad, afraid, surprised, and/or experiencing any one of many other emotions and feelings.

In this example, we're seeing the good kind of wrinkling. The eyebrows are up, letting us know the person is listening and taking in information. This causes the almost straight-lined wrinkling we see on most every listener's forehead. Greg Hartley refers to this setup as the "Request for Approval" eyebrows and wrinkles. For example, if a child asks if they can have a cookie, their eyebrows will be up. When you say, "Yes, you can have one," the child's eyebrows will go back down.

When we see this type of wrinkling along with the regulator and squinting, it tells us the person is putting the conversation on short pause while they interject new information or ask a question.

04: SMALL SMILE (THE SLOW AND TINY SMILE)

A smile, no matter how large or small, is the most potent nonverbal cue in existence. However, the smile is the cue that also lies more than any other. We can use it to tell people everything is fine when we know the situation is circling the drain. That's why it is important to look for the small smile, that little one the person probably doesn't realize they're showing you. That's what we're seeing in the example picture.

As we discussed early in this book, in the late 1800s, French scientist Duchenne de Boulogne discovered that there is a big difference between a real smile and a fake smile: the little wrinkles formed at the sides of the eyes when we smile a real, genuine smile. When we see a fake smile, there are no wrinkles. In this example, we are seeing a real smile. This is not just because the person is squinting. The squinting wrinkles are different; they're big. The real smile wrinkles are small but you can see them fairly easily once you know to look for them.

05: FINGERS LIGHTLY RUBBING TOGETHER

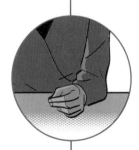

Rubbing your fingers together falls under the adaptor category. Sometimes we use adaptors to relieve built-up stress and tension. Other times, we use these actions to help us keep calm as the excitement around us builds. In this example, we're seeing the interviewer lightly rub their fingers together as an adaptor, but are they stressed or are they excited?

If we take into consideration all the other nonverbal cues we see this individual engaged in, it's safe to say we're most likely seeing stress caused by the anxiety of wanting to move things along a little bit faster. Maybe the needed information for the reviewer has been relayed and the person being reviewed is telling a story that is not relevant to what is going on or is taking up too much time. The reviewer knows they need to cut it off soon but is waiting for an opportunity to do so.

In a similar scenario, you may see someone's leg jiggling under the table when they're trying to hurry another person along with their story without seeming out of line or rude.

CONCLUSION

Now that you have a better understanding of human behavior, you'll never be the same. You'll see deception happen blatantly in front of others and they will completely miss it. You're going to want to interject your newfound knowledge into the middle of things, but take my advice: Don't. Just observe and remember who's being deceptive.

You now know that when someone's arms are crossed or when one's shoulder shrugs, it means nothing specific. When someone tells you it DOES mean something specific, just smile, act normal, and nod your head (with your eyebrows up of course, because supposedly you're taking in new information). When you see someone in panic mode using every adaptor and barrier they have at their disposal, say nothing. Just observe. You're about to learn so much more about that person.

When someone is trying to sell you a used car and they don't break eye contact very often, you now know it's time to shop somewhere else. When you get called to your boss's office and they've leaned forward with their chin over their clasped fingers, you now know there's probably a promotion or a raise marching toward the conversation. Just keep smiling that slow and tiny smile.

Now, take your newfound secret powers, go out into the world, and use them for good!

Scott

RESOURCES

BOOKS

If you'd like to learn about body language and human behavior, in addition to those listed within the References section, here are some books I suggest. All the "Big Guns" read these.

Body Language by Julius Fast

Dangerous Personalities: An FBI Profiler Shows You How to Identify and Protect Yourself from Harmful People by Joe Navarro and Toni Sciarra Poynter

Detecting Lies and Deceit: Pitfalls and Opportunities by Aldert Vrij

The Dictionary of Body Language: A Field Guide to Human Behavior by Joe Navarro

The Ellipsis Manual: Analysis and Engineering of Human Behavior by Chase Hughes

Emotions Revealed: Recognizing Faces and Feelings to Improve Communication and Emotional Life by Paul Ekman

The Face of Man: Expressions of Universal Emotions in a New Guinea Village by Paul Ekman

Find Out Anything from Anyone, Anytime: Secrets of Calculated Questioning From a Veteran Interrogator by James Pyle & Maryann Karinch

Handbook of Methods in Nonverbal Behavior Research by Paul Ekman and Klaus Scherer

How to Spot a Liar: Why People Don't Tell the Truth . . . and How to Catch Them by Greg Hartley & Maryann Karinch

I Can Read You Like a Book: How to Spot the Messages and Emotions People Are Really Sending with Their Body Language by Greg Hartley & Maryann Karinch

The Most Dangerous Business Book You'll Ever Read by Greg Hartley & Maryann Karinch

The Naked Ape: A Zoologist's Study of the Human Animal by Desmond Morris

Nonverbal Communication by Albert Mehrabian

Organization and Pathology of Thought by David Rapaport

Peoplewatching: The Desmond Morris Guide to Body Language by Desmond Morris

The Power of Body Language: How to Succeed in Every Business and Social Encounter by Tonya Reiman

Telling Lies: Clues to Deceit in the Marketplace, Politics, and Marriage by Paul Ekman

The True Believer: Thoughts on the Nature of Mass Movements by Eric Hoffer

Truth and Lies: What People Are Really Thinking by Mark Bowden and Tracey Thomson

Unmasking the Face: A Guide to Recognizing Emotions from Facial Clues by Paul Ekman

What Every BODY Is Saying: An Ex-FBI Agent's Guide to Speed-Reading People by Joe Navarro

Winning Body Language: Control the Conversation, Command Attention, and Convey the Right Message Without Saying a Word by Mark Bowden

WEBSITES

Here are a few websites you can visit for valid information you can trust. Some of these people are scientists and analytical types, so the information they present will be a bit more "researchy."

ScottRouse.com

BodyLanguageTactics.com

TheBehaviorPanel.com

PaulEkman.com

GregHartley.com

DavidMatsumoto.com

Joe Navarro's site: JNForensics.com

Mark Bowden's site: TruthPlane.com

Dr. Albert Mehrabian's site: Kaaj.com/psych

Dr. Nalini Ambady's site: AmbadyLab.Stanford.edu

Uri Hasson's site: HassonLab.com

ChaseHughes.com

REFERENCES

Allen, Bud, and Diana Bosta. *Games Criminals Play: How You Can Profit by Knowing Them*. Rae John Publishers, 2002.

Babiak, Paul, and Robert D. Hare. *Snakes in Suits: When Psychopaths Go to Work*. New York, NY: ReganBooks, 2006.

Bowden, Mark, and Andrew Ford. *Winning Body Language for Sales Professionals: Control the Conversation and Connect with Your Customer—without Saying a Word*. New York, NY: McGraw-Hill Professional, 2012.

Bowden, Mark, and Tracey Thomson. *Truth and Lies: What People Are Really Thinking*. Scarborough, ON, Canada: HarperCollins, 2018.

Ekman, Paul, and Wallace Friesen. *Unmasking the Face*. Old Tappan, NJ: Prentice Hall, 1975.

Ekman, Paul. *Emotions Revealed: Recognizing Faces, Feelings and Their Triggers to Improve Communication and Emotional Life*. Westminster, CO: Times Books, 2003.

Ekman, Paul. *Telling Lies: Clues to Deceit in the Marketplace, Politics, and Marriage*. New York, NY: WW Norton, 2009.

Fast, Julius. *Body Language*. London, England: Pan Books, 1972.

Hare, Robert J. *Without Conscience: The Disturbing World of the Psychopaths among Us*. London, England: Time Warner Paperbacks, 1994.

Hartley, Gregory, and Maryann Karinch. *How to Spot a Liar: Why People Don't Tell the Truth . . . and How You Can Catch Them*. Richmond, England: Crimson Publishing, 2009.

Hartley, Gregory, and Maryann Karinch. *I Can Read You like a Book: How to Spot the Messages and Emotions People Are Really Sending with Their Body Language*. Career Press, 2007.

Hartley, Gregory, and Maryann Karinch. *The Most Dangerous Business Book You'll Ever Read*. 1st ed. Chichester, England: John Wiley & Sons, 2011.

Hughes, Chase. *The Ellipsis Manual: Analysis and Engineering of Human Behavior*. Evergreen Press, 2017.

Morris, Desmond. *Bodytalk: A World Guide to Gestures*. London, England: Jonathan Cape, 2016.

Morris, Desmond. *Naked Ape: A Zoologist's Study of the Human Animal*. Glasgow, Scotland: HarperCollins Distribution Services, 1977.

Morris, Desmond. *Peoplewatching: The Desmond Morris Guide to Body Language*. London, England: Vintage Digital, 2012.

Navarro, Joe, and Marvin Karlins. *What Every BODY Is Saying: An Ex-FBI Agent's Guide to Speed-Reading People*. New York, NY: William Morrow Paperbacks, 2008.

Navarro, Joe. *Dangerous Personalities*. Emmaus, PA: Rodale Press, 2014.

Navarro, Joe. *Louder than Words: Take Your Career from Average to Exceptional with the Hidden Power of Nonverbal Intelligence*. New York, NY: William Morrow, 2010.

Pease, Barbara, and Allan Pease. *The Definitive Book of Body Language: The Hidden Meaning behind People's Gestures and Expressions*. New York, NY: Random House, 2006.

Reiman, Tonya. *Power of Body Language*. New York, NY: Pocket Books, 2008.

Vrij, Aldert. *Detecting Lies and Deceit: Pitfalls and Opportunities*. 2nd ed. Hoboken, NJ: Wiley-Blackwell, 2011.

INDEX

K

L

M

N

O

P

R

S

ACKNOWLEDGMENTS

These are the people I must acknowledge and truly thank.
My beautiful, wonderful, and patient wife, Ambre. My parents,
Dr. Jim and Marilyn Rouse. My sister, Ellen Werner, and my
brother, Mitch Rouse. I can't go without mentioning one of
my mentors, inspirations, and great friends, Greg Hartley. Jason
Rosalia and Shawn Glinter also belong in this group. Thank you
all for your encouragement, love, and help. I must also acknowledge and thank Mark Bowden and Chase Hughes for sharing
their friendship and wisdom. Thank you, Joe Navarro, and sorry
about all the emails. I thank you all from the bottom of my heart.

ABOUT THE AUTHOR

 **SCOTT ROUSE** is a behavior analyst and body language expert. He holds multiple certificates in advanced interrogation training and has trained alongside the Federal Bureau of Investigation, United States Secret Service, United States Military Intelligence, and United States Department of Defense. His extensive training, education, and practice of nonverbal communication has made Scott an expert and consultant to law enforcement and to the United States military, as well as to *Fortune* 500 CEOs, doctors, attorneys, executives, and entertainers. Scott is also a trial consultant and globally popular keynote speaker.